D0008595

JANE GOODALL
A LIFE WITH CHIMPS

Neil Armstrong

Jackie Robinson

Harriet Tubman

Jane Goodall

>>TRAIL BLAZERS

JANE GOODALL
A LIFE WITH CHIMPS

ANITA GANERI

RANDOM HOUSE 🏠 NEW YORK

Text copyright © 2019 by Anita Ganeri
Cover art copyright © 2019 by Luisa Uribe and George Ermos
Interior illustrations copyright © 2019 by Artful Doodlers
Trailblazers logo design by Mike Burroughs

All rights reserved. Published in the United States by Random House Children's Books,
a division of Penguin Random House LLC, New York.

Random House and the colophon are registered trademarks of Penguin Random House LLC.

Visit us on the Web! rhcbooks.com

Educators and librarians, for a variety of teaching tools, visit us at
RHTeachersLibrarians.com

Library of Congress Cataloging-in-Publication Data
Name: Ganeri, Anita, author.
Title: Jane Goodall: a life with chimps / Anita Ganeri.
Description: New York: Random House Children's Books, 2019. | Series: Trailblazers |
Includes index.
Identifiers: LCCN 2019009349 (print) | LCCN 2019009678 (ebook) | ISBN 978-0-593-12410-9
(trade pbk.) | ISBN 978-0-593-12411-6 (lib. bdg.) | ISBN 978-0-593-12412-3 (ebook)
Subjects: LCSH: Goodall, Jane, 1934– —Juvenile literature. | Chimpanzees—Research—
Juvenile literature. | Women primatologists—England—Biography—Juvenile literature.
| Primatologists—England—Biography—Juvenile literature.
Classification: LCC QL31.G58 (ebook) | LCC QL31.G58 G36 2019 (print) |
DDC 590.92—dc23

Created by Stripes Publishing Limited, an imprint of the Little Tiger Group

Printed in the United States of America
10 9 8 7 6 5 4 3 2 1

First Edition

Random House Children's Books supports the First Amendment and celebrates the right to read.

Contents

INTRODUCTION

BREAKING DOWN BARRIERS

One November morning in 1960, a young Jane Goodall trudged wearily up a steep hill in Gombe Stream Game Reserve (now known as Gombe Stream National Park), Tanzania. She had been out and about since dawn, looking for chimpanzees in the thick forest that covered the mountain slopes. Frustratingly, she hadn't seen any signs of them so far, and it was almost midday. Suddenly, she heard rustling in the long grass ahead and spied a large, dark shape. Quickly adjusting her binoculars, she recognized a handsome male chimp she had seen many times before. He was sitting next to a tall, brick-red termite mound, poking a long stalk of grass in and out of a hole.

Each time he pulled the stalk out, he picked something off it with his lips.

It looked as if the chimpanzee was using the grass as a tool to "fish" for termites to eat! Jane knew that she was witnessing something amazing. No one had ever seen this behavior before. No one even knew that chimpanzees used tools—until then, scientists thought only humans did that. The enormity of her discovery took a while to sink in. But what she saw that day in Gombe not only changed her life forever but also changed the course of animal science.

⹀ A MAN'S WORLD ⹀

So, what had brought Jane Goodall to the African
jungle in the first place? As a little girl, her favorite toy
was a stuffed chimpanzee called Jubilee. This cuddly
companion, together with her love of animal stories,
awakened Jane's interest in wild and faraway places. As
she grew older, she began to dream of living and working
among animals in Africa. But, at that time, the field of
scientific research and exploration was very much a
man's world. As Jane later said, "When I was a little girl,
I used to dream as a man, because I wanted to do things
that women didn't do back then, such as traveling to
Africa, living with wild animals, and writing books."

Jane and her friends were expected not to follow
such an adventurous career but to get married and
run a home instead. She was even presented to the
queen at Buckingham Palace as a debutante. She
went to dances and balls, where many of the girls were
hoping to meet a husband. Later, Jane remembered
being surrounded by girls who asked her if she
dreamed of living at the palace and attending on the
queen. The other girls were appalled at Jane's answer:
"Absolutely not—I want to live among wild animals!"

Even when Jane was carrying out her research in Africa, she struggled to be taken seriously, because she was viewed as an unqualified young woman. When her findings made it into the newspapers, the headlines focused on her looks rather than her work. Jane's discoveries were also severely undermined by academics, who were usually men. Jane hadn't been to college, they reminded each other, so what did she know about making accurate observations or keeping detailed notes?

Many academics also criticized her research methods while she was out in the field. When Jane began work at Gombe, there had only been one short study of chimpanzees in the wild. Very little was known about them. Jane took a new, creative approach to her work. Rather than watching the chimpanzees from afar in a cold, clinical way, she spent hours among them, getting to know their habitat, personalities, emotions, and lives. To form a closer bond, Jane gave the chimpanzees names instead of numbers, going against the thinking of the day. Many scientists were horrified. They disapproved of giving animals humanlike qualities, but Jane was determined that each chimpanzee should be recognized as a distinct being. Her way of working brought great rewards. She was able to find out things about chimpanzees that we would never have known otherwise.

Jane came from a family of strong women and had the full support of her mother and grandmothers. In fact, Jane thought that being a woman helped her in some ways. She was able to form good relations with the local people in Gombe. At that time, many African countries were gaining their independence after years of colonization by Western European powers.

After years of fighting, local people were still very wary of European men, but they didn't see Jane as a threat, and they went out of their way to help her.

Colonialism in Africa

In the early part of the 20th century, European countries including Britain, France, and Belgium ruled over most of Africa. This was known as colonialism. The Europeans often took power by force, using newly developed weapons such as machine guns, which the African armies could not match. Africa was rich in resources—including copper, cotton, and diamonds—as well as land for settlement. The European countries were deadly rivals, each interested in building the greatest empire and having control over the most important trade routes. After World War II, however, countries around the world demanded their independence. Over the following decades, either by peaceful negotiations or violent revolutions, almost all of the countries of Africa were freed from European rule.

Primatology

Primatology, Jane's area of expertise, is the scientific study of primates (the group of animals that includes lemurs, lorises, monkeys, and apes). It is a mixture of different sciences, including zoology, anthropology, and psychology. Primates are our closest relatives. By studying them, primatologists hope to be able to come closer to understanding more about human evolution and behavior. Primatologists work in many different places: some conduct experiments in laboratories; some work in zoos, museums, or wildlife parks; and others work in the field, studying primates in their natural environments in the wild.

When Jane first started studying chimpanzees, primatology was a relatively new area of a study, with just a handful of scientists working in the field.

FRANS DE WAAL
(born 1948)
A Dutch primatologist who pioneered the study of cognition (the process of gained knowledge) among primates.

ROBERT M. YERKES
(1876–1956)
An American psychologist who studied human and primate intelligence, particularly among chimpanzees and gorillas.

HANS KUMMER
(1930–2013)
A Swiss zoologist who carried out pioneering field research into the social life of hamadryas baboons.

KINJI IMANISHI
(1902–1992)
An anthropologist who was the first to study wild Japanese monkeys and who helped found the study of primatology in Japan.

Jane's groundbreaking discoveries at Gombe caused a sensation in the scientific world. Until that day in November 1960, scientists had believed that humans were the only living creatures that could make and use tools. It was what set humans apart from other animals, they'd thought. Jane's work was to revolutionize primatology and prove the close links between people and chimpanzees, challenging the uniqueness of human beings.

It took some time for scientists to accept her findings, but since then they have gone on to discover that other animals, including crows, elephants, sea otters, and orangutans, also make and use tools to solve problems and find food.

For Jane, at twenty-six years old, this discovery marked the beginning of a lifetime's work. She was to spend the next forty or so years observing chimpanzees and championing their cause. But all of that was still to come. As she sat on the hillside in Gombe watching a chimpanzee fish for food, she was unaware of the extraordinary impact that her discoveries were about to make on science, and the world.

"The chimpanzee study was—well, it's still going on, and I think it's taught us perhaps more than anything else to be a little humble; that we are, indeed, unique primates, we humans, but we're simply not as different from the rest of the animal kingdom as we used to think."
—Jane Goodall

CHAPTER 1

A CHIMPANZEE NAMED JUBILEE

Valerie Jane Morris-Goodall was born on April 3, 1934, in London, England. Jane's father, Mortimer Morris-Goodall, was an engineer with a passion for racing cars. Her mother, Vanne (pronounced "van"), wrote novels. Her younger sister, Judith (Judy), was born in 1938, on Jane's fourth birthday.

Jane had a happy childhood. The family was not well off, but life was filled with laughter and fun. Soon after she was born, she and her parents moved to a house outside the city, which they shared with a nanny and a bull terrier called Peggy.

Jane was fascinated by animals from a very young age. Her constant companion was a large, stuffed toy chimpanzee named Jubilee, which her father had bought for her when she was just a year old. To her delight, it played music when she pressed its belly. The toy was specially created to celebrate the birth of Jubilee, the first chimpanzee ever born at London Zoo. Before then, all the zoo's chimps had been born in the wild in Africa. Jane's mother's friends were horrified. They thought the toy would frighten Jane and give her nightmares, but they couldn't have been more wrong! From the moment he was given to her, Jubilee became Jane's most treasured possession and never left her side.

That's a lot of slime...

⋝ ANIMAL ADVENTURES ⋜

Jane's fascination with animals began very early
in her life. At around eighteen months old, she dug
up a handful of wriggling worms from the garden,
took them home, and put them under her pillow
when she went to bed. A shocked Vanne spotted
the worms when she came to tuck Jane in. She
explained that Jane couldn't keep them, because
they needed to be in the soil; otherwise they would
die. Jane was disappointed but quickly took the
worms back outside—she hated the idea that any
animal would suffer on her account.

Shortly afterward, Jane and her family went on
a vacation to Cornwall, in southern England, where
they stayed in a house near a rocky seashore. Jane
spent hours on the beach, happily investigating the
rock pools and their fascinating wildlife. One day,
she filled her bucket with seashells and carried it
proudly back to the house. Later, Vanne discovered
bright yellow sea snails crawling all over the walls
and floor of Jane's bedroom! Immediately, the
whole family was ordered to stop whatever they
were doing and come to the rescue.

By the age of five, Jane was already a budding naturalist. Once, Vanne took her to stay with her grandmother (Mortimer's mother, Mrs. Nutt). Jane called her grandmother "Danny Nutt" (Jane couldn't say "Granny" when she was young). Danny Nutt lived in the countryside in an old manor house, where Jane's father had grown up. She kept geese and chickens, and Jane was given the job of collecting the hens' eggs. As the days passed, Jane began to wonder, "How did an egg come out of a chicken?" She couldn't see an opening big enough on the chicken's body. Eventually, her curiosity got the better of her, and she decided to find out for herself.

Clutching Jubilee, she crawled into the henhouse and hid behind a pile of straw in the corner. Then she waited, without moving or making a noise, for a hen to come in to lay an egg. Time passed slowly and uncomfortably until, at last, a hen trotted inside and sat down on the straw. Jane watched intently, hardly daring to breathe, until the hen shuffled forward, a small, round, white object sticking out from between her legs. Suddenly, the egg popped out onto the straw. The hen clucked, shook her feathers, poked the egg with her beak, and then strutted out of the henhouse.

Bursting with excitement, Jane wriggled out of the henhouse, brushed off the straw, and ran to the house to find her mother. She couldn't wait to tell Vanne what an amazing thing she had seen. Back home, however, Vanne and the family had been frantic with worry. It was getting dark, and Jane had been missing for hours. They had searched for her everywhere they could think of and had just called the police when Jane came running in. Vanne was too relieved to punish her. Instead, she took one look at Jane's beaming face, sat down, and listened to her daughter's breathless tale of how a chicken lays an egg.

⋛ WAR IS DECLARED ⋛

In 1939, Mortimer became a full-time race car driver. Jane and her family moved to France, since most of his races took place in mainland Europe. However, their time in France was brief. A few months after they arrived, Adolf Hitler, the leader of Germany, sent troops into Czechoslovakia. With the threat of war looming, it was not safe for the Morris-Goodall family to stay in France. They returned to England and went to stay with Danny Nutt.

Then, on September 3, 1939, England declared war on Germany. The family listened to the news on the radio. Jane was too young to understand what was going on, but it felt frightening.

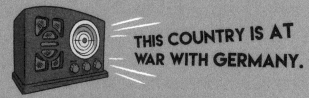

THIS COUNTRY IS AT WAR WITH GERMANY.

Immediately, Mortimer joined the army, while Jane, Judy, and Vanne moved in with Vanne's mother, also known as Danny. She lived in a house called the Birches, in Bournemouth, a seaside town in the south of England. This was where Jane would spend the rest of her childhood and where she still returns today, whenever she is in England.

Hitler and World War II

Adolf Hitler was the head of the Nazi Party. He wanted to restore power to Germany after its defeat in World War I (1914–1918), and his goal was for Germany to rule Europe. As part of his plan, he only wanted certain types of people to live in Germany. He ordered other groups of people who looked different or believed different things, such as Jewish people, to be persecuted and killed.

On September 1, 1939, Adolf Hitler sent his troops into neighboring Poland. In response to Hitler's invasion, Britain and many other countries declared war on Germany. World War II was also fought outside Europe. In 1941, Germany's ally, Japan, attacked the US naval base at Pearl Harbor in Hawaii. The United States declared war on Japan and, in turn, on Germany. After many years of bloodshed, Germany surrendered on May 8, 1945. Japan surrendered on September 2, 1945. After six years, World War II was over. Around sixty-five million people lost their lives, and millions more were injured.

Living in Bournemouth was a lot safer than living in London, which the German air force began bombing in 1940. Even so, the war was never far away from Jane's and her family's thoughts and day-to-day lives. They often heard the droning sound of German planes, and the boom of a bomb exploding somewhere. An air-raid shelter was installed at the Birches, in a room that had once been a maid's bedroom. The shelter was a small, cage-like structure with a low roof that had been issued by the government to thousands of households like theirs. When the air-raid sirens started wailing, usually at night, the family had to leave their beds and huddle together in the cramped, cold shelter, until the "all clear" siren sounded.

Jane and everyone else at the Birches also had their own gas masks in case of a chemical attack, and kept their packed suitcases by the front door in the event they needed to evacuate the house at short notice. During this time, Vanne and the girls had one very lucky escape. One summer, Vanne took them and two friends for a week's vacation just along the coast. After a morning on the beach, it was time to go back to their guest house for lunch. But instead of taking their usual route up the lane, for some reason Vanne insisted that they go the long way around. As they were walking along the beach, they heard a German bomber flying overhead. Vanne yelled to the girls to lie down in the sand. Later, they discovered that one of the bombs had landed halfway up the lane—exactly where they would have been walking if they had taken their usual route.

⋛ BEASTS AT THE BIRCHES ⋛

Despite the war, Jane spent many happy years at the Birches. To her delight, the house had a large, rambling garden, where she played for hours on end. Jane's favorite tree was a big beech tree. She loved it so much that Danny gave it to her, officially, for her tenth birthday. Jane was often found perched on a branch of her tree, reading a book or doing her homework.

Jane also collected a large number of pets, including a tortoise called Johnny Walker, a slow worm called Solomon, a canary called Peter, not to mention several terrapins, guinea pigs, and cats. Jane and Judy also had their own "racing" snails with numbers painted on their shells. The girls kept the snails in a wooden box covered with a piece of glass and with no bottom, so that the snails could feed on fresh dandelion leaves as the girls moved the box around the lawn.

Animal Fact File

Name:	Peter
Animal:	Canary
Behavior:	Slept in a cage but was free to fly around during the day.

⋛ THE ALLIGATOR CLUB ⋚

As well as watching the birds, squirrels, foxes, insects, and spiders that came into the garden, Jane started her own nature club. It was called the Alligator Club and had four members—Jane; Judy; and their two best friends, Sally and Sue Cary, who came to stay at the Birches during the summer breaks. Each girl had to choose

an animal as her code name— Jane was Red Admiral, Sally was Puffin, Sue was Ladybird, and Judy was Trout.

Jane and Judy set up a secret camp in the garden, hidden among the bushes, where the Alligator Club held their meetings. Here, they stored mugs, spoons, and supplies of tea and cocoa in an old trunk. They lit a fire and boiled water for drinking in a tin can balanced on rocks. Sometimes, late at night, the four members of the Alligator Club sneaked out of the house for a midnight feast. During the war, food was rationed in Britain because it was running short. This meant that everyone got a set amount of basic food items every week, and luxury items like sugar and sweets were scarce. The girls' "feasts" were usually made up of the odd cookie or a few crusts of bread left over from meals. The girls didn't mind a bit—they were too excited to be truly hungry.

22

The girls even created a magazine, writing and drawing about the natural world around them. It might have looked something like this.

THE ALLIGATOR CLUB MAGAZINE

EDITION 1

A LETTER FROM RED ADMIRAL

Welcome to the Alligator Club! I hope you like our magazine. There are lots of interesting articles to read, including our new "Animal of the Week" feature. Don't forget to send in any of your own drawings or notes—the more, the merrier. And good luck with our nature quiz. There's fantastic prizes to be won!

Animal of the Week

This week's star animal can sometimes be seen slinking around the camp. It's got a red coat, triangle-shaped ears, and a long bushy tail. Its babies are called cubs. Can you guess what it is?

Answer: A fox

OPENING SOON!
LOOK OUT FOR OUR NEW MUSEUM, OPENING SOON IN THE GREENHOUSE.

Don't miss our next nature walk!
TIME: tomorrow after lunch
PLACE: meet at the secret camp
BRING YOUR NOTEBOOK!

One summer, Jane and her friends turned the greenhouse into a museum, which they filled with shells from the beach and other treasures. Among them was their most prized exhibit: a human skeleton, loaned by Jane's uncle Eric, who was a doctor. Jane and Sally sent the younger girls, Judy and Sue, into the town to persuade passers-by to visit the museum. Visitors were asked to put a donation in a collecting box, and the money raised was given to a local society that rescued old horses.

ADMIT ONE: ALLIGATOR CLUB MUSEUM

⋶ RUSTY AND JANE ⋸

Jane's closest companion at the Birches was Rusty,
a friendly black dog with a white patch on his chest.
Rusty didn't belong to Jane's family—he lived in a
hotel around the corner. As soon as he was let out in
the morning, he would run over to see Jane, and the
pair became inseparable. Jane quickly discovered that
Rusty was excellent at learning commands and tricks.
When she put a biscuit on his nose and said, "Okay,"
he would toss the biscuit into the air, then catch it in
his mouth. Most importantly, Rusty taught Jane that
animals have intelligence, emotions, and personalities—
lessons she would remember all her life.

Animal Fact File

Name: Rusty
Animal: Dog
Behavior: Great at
            learning
            tricks and
            commands.

RUSTY

⋛ DREAMING OF AFRICA ⋛

During the war, Jane had only seen her father for
a few days at a time when he came home on leave.
When she was twelve years old, her parents got
divorced, although they remained good friends. Jane,
Judy, and Vanne carried on living at the Birches,
and Jane attended several different schools. She
was a good student who worked hard and enjoyed
lessons, but she couldn't wait for the school day to
end, so that she could get home. She especially loved
weekends, when she went horseback riding at a local
stable, and school breaks, when she was free to spend
most of her time outdoors with Rusty.

Jane also loved reading and was often found curled
up with a book. One day, Vanne came back from the
library with something that would change Jane's
life. *The Story of Doctor Dolittle* by Hugh Lofting
tells the tale of a doctor who prefers animals to his
human patients, and has the ability to talk to them
in their own language. He travels to Africa, where
he has many extraordinary adventures. Jane was
so enchanted by the book that she read it straight
through three times, the last under the covers with
a flashlight.

She also read all the Tarzan books by Edgar Rice Burroughs, the thrilling tales of a British aristocrat who is brought up in the African jungle by a family of apes. She fell madly in love with the hero, Tarzan, and was very jealous of his companion, who was also named Jane. Now Jane had a new dream, and purpose, to her life. She wanted to live among animals in the wild, and she wanted to go to Africa.

CHAPTER 2

A LETTER FROM AFRICA

At the age of eighteen, Jane graduated from high school. The question was: what was she going to do next? Although she had gotten excellent grades on her final exams, her family did not have enough money to send her to college. All Jane really wanted to do was learn and write about animals, but she had no idea if it was possible to make a living doing that.

[Mother] would say if you really want something, you work hard, you take advantage of opportunity, you never give up, you find a way.

After leaving school, Jane went to stay with a family in Germany. She didn't enjoy the visit much. She tried to learn German, but admitted herself that she wasn't any good at languages.

⋛ WORKING LIFE ⋚

After a few months in Germany, Vanne persuaded Jane to enroll at a secretarial school in London. There, Vanne said, Jane would learn typing and bookkeeping, skills that would enable her to get a job anywhere in the world. Still filled with dreams of working in Africa, Jane agreed. Aged nineteen, she moved to London and set off alone into the big, wide world.

London was a thrilling place to live. Jane spent hours visiting art galleries and museums, including the Natural History Museum, and going to classical music concerts. Because she had very little money, she walked everywhere, and ate as cheaply as she could.

Dinner was often a quarter of a boiled cabbage, followed by an apple or a chocolate cookie! Jane also enrolled in some free evening classes in journalism and English literature—she had always loved poetry and wrote many poems of her own.

After gaining her secretary's diploma, Jane moved back to Bournemouth, where her aunt Olly offered her a job at her physiotherapy clinic. Olly worked with disabled children whose limbs had been damaged by polio and other illnesses, or in accidents. Jane's task was to take down the doctors' notes on each patient and to type up their letters. The work made her realize how lucky she was to be fit and healthy—she never took anything for granted.

After working at Olly's clinic for six months, Jane was offered a job at Oxford University. She found the job itself deadly boring—she worked as a typist and filing clerk for one of the university departments.

> I have been miserable these last few weeks because of the boredom of this foul job.

But at least she was allowed to take Hamlette, her pet hamster, to the office with her every day! In Oxford, Jane shared a house with a group of university students, which she loved. It was almost as good as being a student herself, without the hard work. In her spare time, she liked boating on the river, even though she often fell in.

Jane also attended a couple of Oxford's famous May Balls, wearing a white dress decorated with sequins and swan feathers. She said that she felt like a princess.

By July of 1955, Jane was back in London. She lived in her father's apartment and was glad for the opportunity to get to know him better. A family friend had helped her to find a job at Schofield Productions, a company that made documentary films. It was Jane's responsibility to choose suitable music for the films, but she also learned a great deal about the whole process of filmmaking, and this knowledge would prove useful later in her career. Fascinating though Jane found the work, she was still spending hours reading and dreaming about Africa. She felt as if she were just passing time until she got her lucky break.

⇉ KENYA CALLING ⇇

When the morning mail arrived on Wednesday, December 18, 1956, Jane flicked quickly through it. As she did so, the stamps on one letter caught her eye—they showed elephants and giraffes, animals that lived in Africa.

With trembling hands, Jane tore open the envelope.
Inside was a letter from her old school friend, Marie
Claude Mange (known as "Clo"). Clo wrote that her
parents had bought a farm in Kenya (a country in East
Africa), and that they would all love Jane to visit. Jane
couldn't believe her luck. She had dreamed of going
to Africa for so long, and now, out of the blue, her
chance had come!

But first, Jane had to earn enough money to pay
for her ship fare. Traveling to Africa was expensive,
and she would need a round-trip ticket, which cost
even more. Visitors were not allowed to enter Kenya
on a one-way ticket, and Vanne would never have
allowed it, anyway. Although Jane loved her job at the

film studios, she was not well paid, and living in London was expensive. So, on the same day that she received the letter, she quit her job and returned to the Birches, where she could live rent-free.

To earn money, she began waitressing at a local hotel, saving up all her wages and tips. She hid her money for safekeeping under the carpet in the living room, where Danny always kept her spare cash. Would she ever have enough?

Then one night, after working nonstop for five months, Jane nervously pulled back the carpet and counted her earnings. To her amazement, she found that she had enough for her round-trip ticket and some spending money. She was on her way to Africa—her dream was coming true, at last.

⋝ AFRICA BOUND ⋜

Jane's African adventure began on March 13, 1957.
She booked a passage on a large ocean liner, the *Kenya
Castle*, and was sharing a cabin with five other young
women. Vanne and Uncle Eric came to wave her off at
the London docks. Later, Jane was sure that there must
have been tears as they said goodbye, but could only
remember her feeling of astonishment that the journey
to Africa had finally begun.

Jane thoroughly enjoyed the voyage. She spent
hours up on deck, standing in the bow of the ship,
looking out over the vast expanse of sea. Sometimes,
she glimpsed flying fish, dolphins, and even sharks—a
magical sight. She loved the feel of the sea spray on her
face, especially when the weather turned stormy, and
the other passengers took shelter in their cabins below.

March 15, 1957

It is now 4 p.m. on Thursday,
and I still find it difficult
to believe that I am on my way
to Africa. That is the thing —
AFRICA.

Luckily, as the ship pitched and rolled, Jane never felt seasick.

The *Kenya Castle* sailed down the west coast of Africa, stopping at the Canary Islands. From there, it rounded the Cape of Good Hope, at the southern tip of the continent, stopping off at Cape Town and Durban in South Africa. Its final stop before Mombasa in Kenya was Beira in Mozambique. Jane was fascinated by these places, with their exotic smells, food, and flowers. But not all of these experiences were pleasant or positive ones. In South Africa, Jane came face-to-face with apartheid for the first time. Wherever she went, she saw signs reading "Whites Only." She was horrified.

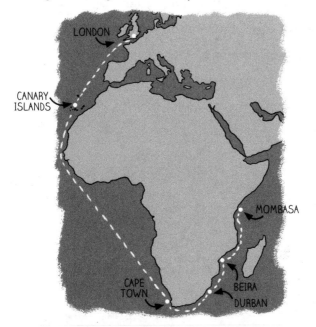

Apartheid

Apartheid was a system in South Africa that kept white people and non-white people apart by law. They had separate schools, restaurants, restrooms, beaches, and separate seats on buses and trains. Non-white people, who made up most of the population, were not considered equal to whites, and were treated very badly. Apartheid lasted from around 1948 to 1991. Following talks with the African National Congress (ANC), the leading anti-apartheid movement, in 1990 the government released several key ANC leaders, including Nelson Mandela, from prison. In 1994, South Africa held its first multiracial elections. The ANC won, and on May 10, Nelson Mandela was sworn in as South Africa's first black president.

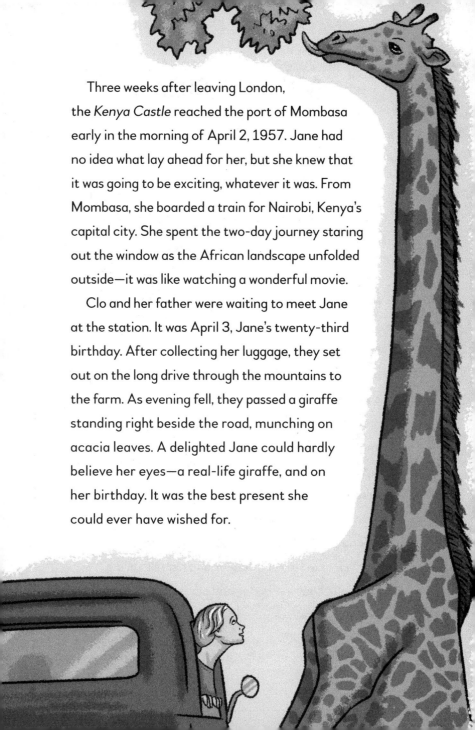

Three weeks after leaving London, the *Kenya Castle* reached the port of Mombasa early in the morning of April 2, 1957. Jane had no idea what lay ahead for her, but she knew that it was going to be exciting, whatever it was. From Mombasa, she boarded a train for Nairobi, Kenya's capital city. She spent the two-day journey staring out the window as the African landscape unfolded outside—it was like watching a wonderful movie.

Clo and her father were waiting to meet Jane at the station. It was April 3, Jane's twenty-third birthday. After collecting her luggage, they set out on the long drive through the mountains to the farm. As evening fell, they passed a giraffe standing right beside the road, munching on acacia leaves. A delighted Jane could hardly believe her eyes—a real-life giraffe, and on her birthday. It was the best present she could ever have wished for.

⋛ LIVING THE DREAM ⋜

Jane spent a few magical weeks on Clo's farm, walking in the mountains and watching the birds and other wildlife.

Right from the moment I got here, I felt at home.

But she didn't want to outstay her welcome, and she had been brought up to fend for herself. Thanks to her uncle Eric, she managed to get a job in Nairobi as a secretary for a British company. The work itself was very boring, but at least she was earning her own money while she tried to find a way of working with animals and staying in Africa. Though she had bought an open return ticket to adhere to Kenya's government requirements, she didn't plan on sailing back to England anytime soon! As luck would have it, she did not have very long to wait before an opportunity arose.

At a party in Nairobi, Jane found herself telling a friend all about her hopes and plans. "If you are interested in animals," the friend replied, "you must meet Louis Leakey."

Louis Leakey

Louis Leakey was a famous paleoanthropologist, a scientist who studies early human beings. He was born and brought up in Kenya, his parents having traveled to  Africa from Britain to work as missionaries, teaching people about Christianity. As a teenager, Louis found some stone tools made by early humans. This sparked off a lifelong interest in studying the origins of human beings. With his wife, Mary, he began to hunt for fossils of early humans in the Olduvai Gorge in Tanzania. Finally, in the early 1960s, they discovered fossil bones believed to belong to the earliest ancestors of modern humans. Louis's work helped changed scientists' views of how and where human beings had begun. Before his findings, it was thought that the earliest humans had come from Asia, rather than Africa.

Louis was the head of the Coryndon Museum of Natural History (now called the National Museum of Kenya). Without delay, Jane made an appointment to meet him. She was shown to his untidy office, which was strewn with piles of paper, fossil bones and teeth, stone tools, and a large cage containing a tiny mouse and her minute babies.

On a tour of the museum, Louis fired question after question at Jane, most of which she managed to answer. Impressed by Jane's knowledge and enthusiasm, Louis immediately offered her a job as his secretary.

What's herpetology?

The study of reptiles and amphibians.

What's ichthyology?

The study of fish.

What are you doing in Africa?

Trying to find a way to live among animals!

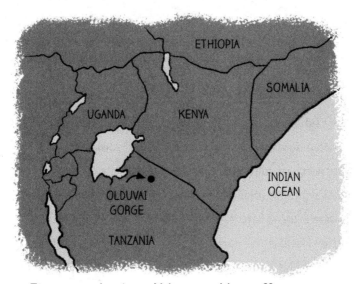

Every year, Louis and Mary would set off on a three-month expedition to the Olduvai Gorge to dig for fossils, hoping to unearth the bones of early humans. Soon after Jane began working at the museum, they invited her and another English girl, Gillian, to join them. Jane was thrilled. At that time, this remote place was known to very few people, apart from the local Maasai tribes. There was no road, nor even a track, leading to the gorge. As they got closer, Jane and Gillian had to sit on the roof of the jeep, looking out for the faint tire marks left by the Leakeys the year before. They finally reached Olduvai as it was getting dark, quickly set up camp, and built a fire. Later, Jane heard the distant roar of lions, and the strange giggling calls of hyenas. She had never been so happy in her life.

At Olduvai, Jane's main job was to dig for fossils—it was fascinating but exhausting work in the baking sun. For hours each day, Jane chipped away at the hard soil with a hunting knife. When she found something of interest, usually the remains of a prehistoric animal, she used dental picks to pry it gently out of the ground. Jane later wrote: "I will always remember the first time I held in my hand the bone of a creature that had walked the earth millions of years before. I had dug it up myself. A feeling of awe crept over me."

⋛ CHIMPANZEE CHALLENGE ⋚

Back in Nairobi, Jane returned to her job at the museum. She was happy enough, and learning a great deal, but she still longed to be back in the outdoors, working with living animals rather than the fossils and dead specimens that filled the museum's dusty cases.

Meanwhile, Louis began to tell Jane about his great interest in chimpanzees, especially a group he knew of in Tanzania. Chimps are very closely related to humans. If he learned about how chimps behave, Louis believed, he could find out more about our earliest ancestors.

But the only way to do this was for someone to study chimps in the wild (wild chimps only live in Africa), and it wouldn't be an easy task. The chimps' forest habitat was remote and risky, and the person chosen would need to be physically strong, as well as willing to spend months away from civilization. Louis already knew exactly the right person for the job, but he never got the chance to make the offer. One day, Jane blurted out, "Louis, I wish you wouldn't keep talking about it, because that's just what I want to do." "Jane," Louis replied, "I've been waiting for you to tell me that."

Jane was stunned. She had no scientific training and had not been to college, so she had never imagined that Louis would choose her for his project. That said, she was ready to set off at once, if need be! First, though, Louis needed to get government permission for the study, and to raise some much-needed funds. While he did this, he advised Jane to learn all she could about chimpanzees—back in England.

CHAPTER 3

MEETING DAVID GREYBEARD

As soon as she reached England, Jane began to read everything she could about chimps. The more she read, the more she realized how intelligent they are. At that time, almost nothing was known about their natural behavior. Only one scientist, an American psychologist named Dr. Henry W. Nissen, had tried watching them in the wild. In 1923, he spent just two and half months in the forests of French Guinea, but had very little luck locating any chimps. He and his team of porters made such a racket that the chimps fled when they heard them coming.

Apart from reading, Jane also spent hours observing the chimps at London Zoo, but was deeply shocked at the terrible conditions they lived in. The male chimp, Dick, had been shut in his tiny cement cage for so long that he had gone mad. Hunched miserably in the corner, he spent his days fiddling with his fingers, and opening and closing his mouth.

Meanwhile, in Kenya, Louis had at last found funding for the trip, and organized a work permit for Jane. She would be heading to the remote Gombe Stream Game Reserve (now Gombe Stream National Park) in Tanzania, where it was thought 160 chimps lived. There was just one snag. In those days, the authorities would not allow Jane to travel by herself. She needed a companion, but whom should she choose? To Jane's delight, her mother, Vanne, volunteered to go with her for a few months, to help her settle in. Jane couldn't think of anyone better.

Many people thought that Louis was making a mistake in choosing Jane for the project. She had no formal training and did not look strong enough to survive in the forest for a week, let alone several months. Jane—and Louis—were to prove them all wrong!

SO CLOSE, YET SO FAR

With growing excitement, Jane and Vanne boarded a plane for Nairobi, where Louis met them and took them to a hotel. In Nairobi, they were kept very busy, packing everything they needed for their expedition: tents; bedding; cooking equipment; cans of food; clothes; binoculars; and, of course, plenty of notebooks.

Like her daughter, Vanne was thrilled to be back in Africa. She had visited once before when Jane was working at the museum. Vanne loved meeting Jane's friends—both human and animal—and had quickly made friends of her own.

Bernard Verdcourt, a botanist from the museum, drove Jane and Vanne to Kigoma, the nearest town to Gombe. Louis was to stay behind, in order to carry on his research. It was a daunting 746 miles (1,200 km) from Nairobi, mostly along rough tracks. The jeep they traveled in was so overloaded that it swayed dangerously if Bernard drove too fast, and there was barely room to sit inside. To make matters worse, swarms of tsetse flies followed the car and attacked the passengers whenever they stopped, or on the three occasions when the car broke down. Despite this, they reached Kigoma on July 8, 1960, three bumpy days after setting out. Gombe was tantalizingly close, but now they faced yet another delay. Violent riots had broken out on the other side of Lake Tanganyika. It wasn't safe for Jane and Vanne to leave Kigoma—they would have to sit and wait. Refugees from the fighting began pouring into the town, in desperate need of food and shelter. To make room, Jane and Vanne moved out of their hotel and set up their tent in the grounds of the local prison.

They also volunteered to help feed the refugees. One night, they made 2,000 Spam sandwiches (Spam is a type of canned cooked ham).

⩾ GOMBE, AT LAST ⩽

At long last, on July 16, 1960, the authorities gave Jane and Vanne permission to leave. A government motorboat was ready to take them across the lake. About an hour later, the boat reached the edge of the Gombe reserve and headed for a pebbly beach. As Jane jumped out of the boat, she struggled to take it all in. She loved the place as soon as she saw it, but she was nervous about what lay ahead, and did not want to let Louis down.

With the help of a game ranger as well as their cook, Dominic, they set up camp close to the beach. Home for the next few months was an old army tent, which Jane and Vanne shared. There was a separate area for washing at the back, and a deep hole in the ground, surrounded by a palm-leaf fence, for their toilet. There was also a makeshift kitchen made from a few wooden poles topped with a straw roof. Dominic pitched his tiny tent nearby. Their little camp was rough and ready, but to Jane it felt like being in paradise. As Jane said:

Everything was interesting.

Gombe Stream National Park

Gombe Stream is one of the smallest national parks in Tanzania, covering just over 31 sq. mi. Stretching along the shore of Lake Tanganyika, it is a rugged region of steep valleys, hills, and forests. Though best known for its chimps, Gombe is also home to many other primates, including olive baboons, red-tailed and red colobus monkeys, vervet monkeys, and blue monkeys. There are also bush pigs, antelopes, snakes, and more than 200 species of birds. For an unforgettable experience, visitors to the park can travel from Kigoma by water taxi or motorboat, then take a guided walk deep into the forest to sit with and observe the chimps.

⋚ CHIMPANZEE WATCH ⋚

As soon as she arrived, Jane was desperate to start work. Equipped only with a pair of binoculars, a notebook, and a pencil, she set out into the mountains, accompanied by a local guide, while Vanne stayed in camp. On the first day, they spotted two chimps feeding high up in a tree. But the chimps quickly leaped down and ran away.

About a week later, the guide led Jane to a large tree full of round, red fruit. From her lookout a little way away, Jane watched a group of chimps arrive at the tree and feast on the fruit, but she was too far away to see very much.

Ever get the feeling you're being watched?

Primate, Monkey, or Ape?

There are more than three hundred species of primates. They all share many features, including large brains compared to the size of their bodies, forward-facing eyes, and flexible limbs and hands for grasping. But, while monkeys and apes (chimps, bonobos, gorillas, orangutans, and gibbons) are both primates, monkeys are not the same as apes. Here's how to tell them apart:

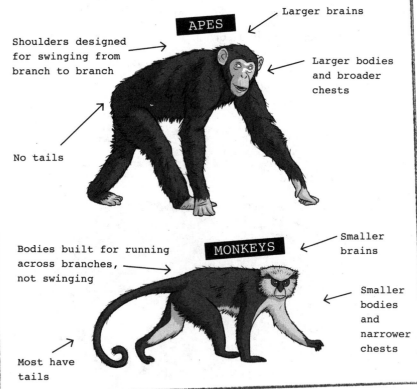

APES

Larger brains

Shoulders designed for swinging from branch to branch

Larger bodies and broader chests

No tails

MONKEYS

Smaller brains

Bodies built for running across branches, not swinging

Smaller bodies and narrower chests

Most have tails

Over the next few months, Jane's frustration grew. Sometimes, she didn't see any chimps for days, and when she did, she couldn't get close enough to observe them properly. So as not to startle the chimps, Jane wore clothes that blended in with the forest, and sat patiently for hours. The minute she tried to move nearer, the chimps scampered off. She was getting worried that if she didn't get results soon, Louis would have to cancel the project, and she would have to leave Gombe.

Sweater

Food and drink

Notebook and pens

BEANS BEANS

Binoculars

Sleeping bag

Bagged lunch

To make matters worse, Jane and Vanne fell ill with malaria. They had been told that there was no malaria at Gombe, and so hadn't brought any medicine along. For two weeks, they couldn't do anything but lie in their beds, side by side, at times burning with fever, at others shivering with cold. For four days, Vanne's temperature rose as high as 105 degrees. She was lucky to survive.

Murderous Malaria

Malaria is a very serious disease, most common in tropical places. It is spread by a certain kind of mosquito. The mosquito's bite injects a parasite into the blood, which causes damage to the blood and liver. Symptoms are like those of a terrible flu—headaches, high fever, chills, and vomiting. Up to 500 million people catch malaria each year, with around two million people dying. Most of these deaths happen in Africa; many of those who die are children. There is no vaccine for malaria, but there are medicines to prevent you from catching the disease, and sprays for killing the mosquitoes. Special nets can be spread over beds to stop the mosquitoes from biting at night. Unfortunately, many poorer people cannot afford these simple safeguards.

CHIMPS AT THEIR PEAK

As soon as she felt well enough, Jane returned to work. She got into the habit of waking up early, having a quick breakfast of bread and coffee, and then setting off to search for chimps while it was still cool. By now, she had persuaded the guides to let her explore on her own. That way, she argued, she could go at her own pace, and would make less noise. Climbing slowly, often through thick bush, she headed up the steep, rocky slope opposite the campsite, which she named "the Peak." From this viewpoint, hundreds of feet up, she could see a large group of about fifty chimps moving around in the nearby trees. Over the next few months, she observed them closely and learned more about the group—which trees they fed on, which fruit they ate, how they interacted with each other, and how the young chimps liked to play.

Spotter's Guide
to Chimpanzees

Scientific name: Pan troglodytes

Animal type: Mammal

Found in: Forests in Africa

Diet in the wild: Leaves, fruit, insects, monkeys, honey, eggs

Lifespan in the wild: 45 years

Height: 25–37 in. (64–94 cm)

Weight: Males 75–154 lb. (34–70 kg); females 57–110 lb. (26–50 kg)

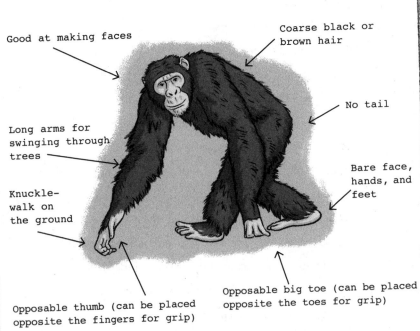

Good at making faces

Coarse black or brown hair

No tail

Long arms for swinging through trees

Bare face, hands, and feet

Knuckle-walk on the ground

Opposable thumb (can be placed opposite the fingers for grip)

Opposable big toe (can be placed opposite the toes for grip)

Little by little, the chimps got used to Jane, although she still could not get very close. It was a chimpanzee that she had named David Greybeard who changed all that. One evening, when Jane got back from the Peak, an excited Dominic reported that a big male chimpanzee had come into camp and fed on fruits from the palm tree. Then the chimpanzee had gone to Jane's tent and eaten some bananas.

The next day, Jane stayed in camp, hoping for another visit. Sure enough, at around 4 p.m., a dark shape appeared out of the undergrowth. She recognized it immediately—it was David Greybeard. More visits followed. Each time, David fed on palm fruits, then helped himself to the bananas Jane put out for him. Then, one day, a thrilling thing happened—he came up to Jane and took a banana out of her hand.

Soon, the other chimps were letting Jane come closer and closer, though she was always careful not to startle or upset them. She knew that chimps don't like being stared at—they find it threatening—so she looked away if they came near. If she noticed them staring at her, she squatted down on the ground, like a chimp, pretending to look for grubs to eat.

⋝ TERMITE FISHING ⋜

It was also David who led Jane to make her two most important discoveries. For a long time, scientists believed that chimps were herbivores that only ate plants. Then, one day, Jane noticed David and some of the other chimps sitting high up in a tree. David was holding something pink, which turned out to be a dead bush piglet. To her amazement, Jane realized that the chimps were feeding on the piglet. This proved, for the first time, that chimps were omnivores—they ate meat as well as plants.

Two weeks later, Jane saw something even more astonishing. One morning, near the Peak, Jane spotted David through her binoculars, sitting by a termite mound (termites are tiny, ant-like insects).

As she watched, David picked up a blade of grass and poked it into a hole in the mound. Then, he carefully pulled the grass out again, and picked something off it with his lips. He repeated this several times, using a new blade when the old one got bent. When David had gone, Jane went over to the termite mound to take a closer look. She pushed a blade of grass into the mound, then pulled it out. It was covered in termites. David had been using the grass to "fish" for termites. Another day, she saw David and another chimp, Goliath, use small twigs for fishing, having first stripped off the leaves.

DISCOVERY ONE: chimps are omnivores.*

DISCOVERY TWO: chimps use tools.*

*Though not quite like this.

Jane had never dreamed of witnessing anything so exciting. The chimps were using tools to collect food! It was a groundbreaking discovery. Until then, scientists had believed that only humans could make and use tools. Back in Nairobi, Louis was thrilled to hear Jane's news. Now more than ever, he knew that she had been the right person for the job. He sent her a telegram that read:

```
Ah! We must now redefine
"man," redefine "tool,"
or accept chimpanzees as
humans.
                      [END]
```

CHAPTER 4

DR. GOODALL, I PRESUME?

At just twenty-six years old, Jane revolutionized the way scientists thought about chimps, though not everyone was happy. Some scientists believed that toolmaking set humans apart from other animals, and now Jane was showing them otherwise. They tried to question her findings, claiming that she did not have the professional training to produce accurate notes and observations. Some even suggested that Jane had staged the whole thing by training the chimps to go termite fishing! Luckily, none of the criticism held her back. In fact, because of Jane's breakthroughs, Louis was able to apply, successfully, to the National Geographic Society in the United States for a grant to fund more research. It meant that Jane could stay at Gombe for another year.

"More and more often, I found myself thinking, *This is where I belong. This is what I came into this world to do.*"
—Jane Goodall

In the meantime, Jane's mother, Vanne, decided to return to England. While Jane was out studying chimps, Vanne had set up a small clinic for local people, giving out basic medicines and dressing wounds. She had brought some medical supplies with her, and her brother, Eric, sent her more from England. The clinic was a success, with people traveling long distances to see Vanne. Jane was going to miss her mother, for her wonderful company and for the relations she had built up within the community.

But Jane didn't have time to feel lonely once Vanne left. Dominic's wife and daughter came to live in camp, and Louis also sent his trusted boat driver, Hassan, with his wife and family. Guests visited on a regular basis, and Jane also learned Swahili, the local language. And then, of course, there was her work.

⋝ NAME THAT CHIMP ⋜

Jane's hours of patient watching and waiting were really paying off. The chimps were overcoming their fear of her, and allowing her to get closer. She learned to recognize individual chimps and gave them names instead of numbers, as scientists normally did. Among them were David Greybeard, Goliath, Mr. McGregor, and Flo.

Animal Fact File

Name: David Greybeard

Animal: Chimpanzee

Distinguishing features:

- Thick, white beard
- Calm and gentle

Animal Fact File

Name: Flo

Animal: Chimpanzee

Distinguishing features:

- Ragged ears and large nose
- Gentle, caring mother

Animal Fact File

Name: Mr. McGregor

(Named after the grumpy gardener in
Beatrix Potter's Peter Rabbit books.)

Animal: Chimpanzee

Distinguishing features:

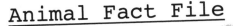

- Bald head, neck, and shoulders
- Grumpy and bad-tempered

Animal Fact File

Name: Goliath

Animal: Chimpanzee

Distinguishing features:

- Named for his large size
- Very strong and agile

≡ CHIMPANZEE BEHAVIOR ≡

It was easy to spot the chimps' different physical features. But Jane was also learning about their distinctive personalities, emotions, and intelligence. She was determined to find out more about these differences, and how their complex society worked.

Jane saw that a group of chimps was made up of many males and females. The chimps generally stayed within a home territory, which they guarded fiercely. An adult male was the leader of the pack and spent years in charge. When he became too old and weak, the younger males fought to take his place. In the group Jane got to know, Goliath was the leader, until he was replaced by Mike. Unusually, Mike had used brains, not brawn, to rise through the ranks.

Flo was the top female. She often brought her latest baby, Flint, into camp with her, looking for bananas. This allowed Jane to observe close-up how a baby chimpanzee develops. Like a human baby, a baby chimpanzee relies on its mother for milk, and to keep it safe. For the first six months, Flint clung to Flo's belly, and later rode on her back. Jane saw that Flo was a devoted mother, often cuddling and tickling Flint.

As Flint grew up, and spent more time playing with other young chimps, his mother still kept a close watch. If she thought the others were being too rough with him, she charged over to threaten them.

More discoveries followed. Often, during the rainy season, Jane glimpsed the chimps huddled together under the trees, looking cold, damp, and miserable. But she also saw them having fun. One stormy day, she noticed a group of chimps in a tree. As torrential rain began to fall, the males left their shelter and started to climb up a nearby hill. At the top, as the thunder rumbled, they swaggered and hooted, then charged back down the hill again. Once at the bottom of the hill, they began their "rain dance" all over again.

Come rain or shine, most of Jane's days were spent in the forest. In the evening, she returned to camp, where Dominic had dinner ready. After eating, she took out her little notebooks in which she had scribbled down everything that she had seen in the day. Then she wrote up her notes, more legibly, in her journal, while they were still fresh in her mind. In time, she started using a small tape recorder so that she could keep her eyes on the chimps all the time. She bought an old typewriter for typing up her notes.

But life at Gombe was not all smooth sailing. Jane's work was risky, and she often faced danger. One day, as she walked through the forest in the pouring rain, she saw a chimpanzee hunched on the ground just ahead. Quickly, she stopped and crouched down. Then she heard a sound coming from above. Looking up, she saw Goliath staring down at her, shrieking and shaking a branch threateningly. Another chimpanzee came up behind her.

Soon, she was
surrounded,
and she was
scared. Suddenly,
one of the chimps
charged toward her,
bristling with rage.
Still Jane didn't move.
The chimp slammed his hand into the back
of Jane's head, then ran off into the bush,
followed by the others. Jane was badly
shaken—a male chimpanzee was three
times stronger than an adult man and
could easily have done her serious harm.
It taught her that, though the chimps
were no longer afraid of her, they had
not yet learned to accept her.

Close Relations

Chimps are more closely related to humans
than they are to gorillas. It's true! They
share almost 99 percent of our DNA (the
material that determines how a living
thing will look and function).
Here are ten ways in which
a chimpanzee is just like you:

1. Chimps have similar skeletons,
   nervous systems, muscles, and
   hands with thumbs.

2. Chimps use their senses of
   sight, smell, hearing, taste,
   and touch to experience the world.

3. Chimps are intelligent,
   with large brains for
   their body size.

4. Chimps can recognize
   themselves in a
   mirror—most animals can't.

5. Chimps show their emotions, like happiness, sadness, and fear.

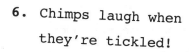

6. Chimps laugh when they're tickled!

7. Chimps use body language to communicate.

8. Chimps sometimes use tools to catch their food.

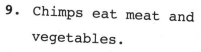

9. Chimps eat meat and vegetables.

10. Chimps spend the first five years of their lives close to their mothers.

⋝ MEETING HUGO ⋜

By now, news of Jane's trailblazing discoveries had reached people around the world. In the spring of 1961, an editor from the National Geographic Society visited Louis in Nairobi, and explained that the magazine wanted to run a story about Jane's work, with photographs showing her with the chimps. Neither Louis nor Jane was keen. Jane was worried that a photographer would disrupt her work and destroy the fragile trust that she was building up with the chimps. But it was difficult for them to say no, especially since the Society was funding Jane's research.

The Society sent out a photographer, but the woman that they had chosen found the working conditions in Gombe too challenging. Next, the editor suggested that Jane take the photographs herself, but the camera they gave her was too complicated to use. Finally, Jane suggested that her sister, Judy, come to Gombe and take the photos. Judy was not a professional photographer, but she understood Jane's work and the importance of not interfering with it. Besides, she looked a lot like Jane, which made it more likely the chimps would accept her. Unfortunately, Judy arrived in late August, at the start of the rainy season. While Jane loved having Judy with her, the weather ruined Judy's chances of taking any photos. The photos she managed to take, several months later, were sadly not good enough for the magazine to use.

Instead, the National Geographic Society sent a man named Hugo van Lawick to take photographs and film Jane for a documentary. Born in Indonesia, Hugo, the son of a Dutch baron, had lived in Australia and England as a boy. He now specialized in photographing African wildlife. Despite being highly recommended byLouis, Jane was not so sure about Hugo. At first, she would only allow him to take photographs in camp, and not out in the field. Jane soon realized, however, that Hugo not only took brilliant photographs, but the two of them had lots in common. For a start, they had both been fascinated by animals since they were very young. Quickly, they became good friends, talking for hours about the chimps.

Say banana!

Hugo made several more trips to Gombe, and in time, he and Jane fell in love. On December 26, 1963, while Jane was back at the Birches in Bournemouth, she received a telegram. It was from Hugo, asking her to marry him. Jane said yes immediately, and their wedding took place on March 28, 1964, in London. It was a very happy day. The top of their wedding cake was decorated with a little clay figure of David Greybeard. Color portraits of David, Goliath, Flo, and many other Gombe chimps looked down on the human guests from the walls.

⋛ DR. JANE ⋛

By the early 1960s, Jane had become the world's
leading expert on chimpanzee research, and her
fame was growing fast. In August 1963, *National
Geographic* magazine ran its first article about her,
titled "My Life Among Wild Chimpanzees." Illustrated
with Hugo's photographs, it was mailed to around
three million readers. Then, in December 1965,
an hour-long documentary film about Jane was
broadcast on American TV. Also filmed by Hugo, it
was called *Miss Goodall and the Wild Chimpanzees*.
The millions of viewers who watched it were
captivated by the chimps, and by Jane.

Meanwhile, Louis had arranged for Jane to study for a PhD (doctor of philosophy) at Cambridge University in England. This would help to get her research taken more seriously by scientists and academics. She began her studies in January 1962, and spent several years dividing her time between Cambridge and Gombe. She couldn't wait to get back to the chimps, and worried they wouldn't recognize her on her return. But she knew how much trouble Louis had taken to get her a university placement, and she worked very hard. In 1965, she received her PhD in ethology (the study of animal behavior)—she had written her thesis on the behavior of free-living chimpanzees. She was now Dr. Jane.

CHAPTER 5

GOOD DAYS AND BAD DAYS

One of Jane's great hopes for Gombe was to set up a research center where students could come from around the world to do research and fieldwork. Her own workload had grown so much that she already had two assistants, but there was always more to be done. Now, her newfound fame meant that her dream might come true.

She applied to the National Geographic Society for funding, and, to her delight, the Society agreed. Construction began in December 1964, and by early 1965, the Gombe Stream Research Center was up and running.

The first buildings were made from aluminum covered with grass and bamboo. There was a large working area, sleeping quarters, a kitchen, and a storage area for bananas. There was also a building for Jane and Hugo to live in. It was thrilling to see it take shape.

As news of the center spread, applications began to pour in. Most of the successful candidates initially came for a year, but many were keen to stay longer. The center quickly expanded, with more housing for students—complete with screens over the windows to stop the chimps from climbing in—and a dining area built near the beach. In the evenings, the students gathered here to eat a meal and give talks about their research, or enjoy a weekly movie night.

Jane was incredibly proud of the research center and the work that it was doing. But, there was a downside to its success. To raise extra funds for the center, she found herself spending more and more time away from Gombe and her beloved chimps. She traveled abroad on lecture tours, often speaking to sell-out audiences, and she also wrote articles and books. It was always a wrench to leave Gombe, and a great joy to be back.

Polio Outbreak

In 1966, tragedy struck Gombe when a polio epidemic broke out among the chimps. Polio is an infection that can cause damage to the limbs. The chimps may have caught polio from humans, as chimps and humans can suffer from many of the same diseases. Jane contacted Louis, who arranged for a delivery of the polio vaccine, which they gave to the chimps in bananas. But for some of the chimps, it was too late. Six chimps died, including Mr. McGregor, one of the first chimps Jane had met at Gombe. Others were left permanently disabled. Jane was devastated.

FAMILY LIFE

The year 1967 was a special one in Jane's life. She and Hugo had a baby son, named Hugo Eric Louis. Until he was three, he had been known as "Little Hugo," but from then on, everyone called him by his nickname of "Grub." Jane's African friends joked that she should have called him "Simba," which means "lion" in the Swahili language. Just before he was born, Jane and Hugo were camping in the Ngorongoro Crater,

famous for its wildlife, especially its lions. One evening, three young male lions visited the camp and ripped open several of their tents. Hugo used the jeep to herd the lions gently away, but the tents were too badly damaged to sleep in, so Hugo and Jane moved to a little log cabin nearby. They'd be much more comfortable in there, once they'd managed to get past the large male lion lying on the veranda! The lion had been feasting on an antelope and was digesting his meal. Eventually, he moved off, and they were able to get into the cabin.

The first few years of Grub's life were spent on the plains of the Serengeti—where Hugo was busy filming hyenas, lions, and wild dogs—or back at Gombe. At Gombe, Jane and Hugo had to be careful to keep Grub away from the chimps. After all, chimps are hunters, and their favorite prey is other primates. Jane had heard two reports of chimps in the local area killing human babies for food, and she was taking no chances. Before Grub could walk, they built him a special "cage" in their house with his crib inside. It was painted bright blue, with colorful birds and stars hanging from the top of the cage. Inside, Grub was safe from harm but could see everything that was going on, even though he was never very fond of the chimps! Once Grub began to walk, he no longer wanted to be in his cage. Jane and Hugo built a new house by the lake shore, with a large, screened-in veranda, where Grub could play.

While Grub was small, Jane spent very little time with the chimps. She was director of the research center, but it was the students and field staff who went into the forests to observe the animals. In the mornings, Jane worked in her office in the house by the lake, writing reports and articles. Then, after lunch, she spent the rest of the day looking after Grub.

Jane believed that watching the chimps, especially Flo, had taught her a lot about being a good mother. Flo was loving, patient, and playful, and her children were confident and sociable. From her, Jane learned that having a child should be fun. She and Grub went for walks, swam in the lake, or simply sat and played. She felt that she had Flo to thank for being a better mother.

Sadly, Jane's marriage to Hugo was suffering. They began spending more time apart—Hugo on filming assignments, and Jane on lecture tours. In 1974, when Grub was seven, they decided to divorce, although they stayed good friends.

⋝ LEAKEY AND THE TRIMATES ⋜

While Jane and Hugo were busy being parents and building the center, one person was missing—Louis Leakey. Louis had not visited Jane in Gombe, because he did not want to get in the way of her work, and later, ill health made it difficult for him to travel there. But the two kept in constant touch by letter and telegram, and Louis could not have been prouder of Jane and all that she had achieved.

Over the years, Leakey had supported two other pioneering primatologists—Dian Fossey and Birutė Galdikas. Like Jane, these women studied primates in their natural habitats. Dian's area of expertise was gorillas, and Birutė's was orangutans. Louis believed that women had more patience than men, and so made better observers. He told Dian and Birutė about Jane, and the importance of carrying out research into great apes.

The three women only met very occasionally to give lectures and talk about their work. Dian and Birutė referred to Jane as the "pioneer," because she had led the way for them to follow in her footsteps. Though the women were not close friends, the newspapers gave them a variety of nicknames, including the "Trimates" and "Leakey's Angels."

Louis had made several important discoveries of his own over the years. He convinced the scientific community that not only did our human ancestors evolve over one million years earlier than previously thought, but that these early relatives lived in Africa rather than Asia. While Louis was known as a showman, prone to exaggeration and sweeping statements, his wife Mary was a meticulous scientist. She continued to excavate fascinating finds, including uncovering a 3.75-million-year-old hominin fossil (an ancient human relative).

Louis was also great friends with Jane's mother, Vanne. On October 1, 1972, he died of a heart attack in London. Vanne was with him near the end. He was sixty-nine years old. Jane had lost her mentor and great friend. The best way to honor his memory, she decided, was to work even harder than before.

"What is it that really makes us, us? It's our collective intelligence. It's our ability to write things down, our language and our consciousness."
—Louis Leakey

Dian Fossey

Born in San Francisco, California, in 1932,
Dian was fascinated by animals from a young
age. Like Jane, she dreamed of visiting
Africa and studying African wildlife.
In 1963, determined to make her dream a
reality, Dian took out a bank loan and
traveled to Kenya, ready to embark on
a tour of the continent.

At Olduvai Gorge, she met Louis Leakey. He
showed her his recent excavations and spoke
about the need for further studies on great
apes. Four years later, with her loan repaid
and Louis's support, Dian relocated to Africa—
she was to head up a project studying mountain
gorillas in the Virunga Mountains in the
Democratic Republic of Congo. But Dian faced a
rocky road ahead. Less than a year after she'd
arrived, she returned from a day studying the
gorillas in the forest to discover a large
group of armed soldiers waiting in her camp.
They told her to leave Virunga and not to
return. Disheartened but not defeated, Dian
restarted her studies, founding Karisoke
Research Center in Rwanda. She went on to make
many important discoveries about gorillas, as
well as writing the bestselling book *Gorillas
in the Mist*. She found out:

- Gorillas have strong family bonds, and mourn each other's deaths.
- Chest thumping is a signal of strength and power.
- Gorillas are vegetarian and spend most of the day searching for food.
- At night, gorillas bed down in nests made of branches and leaves.

Dian shared a special bond with Digit, so named as one of his fingers was injured. Tragically, Digit was killed by poachers in 1977.

Birutė Galdikas

Born in Germany to Lithuanian parents, Birutė moved to Canada when she was just two years old. In college, Birutė studied psychology and zoology before gaining a master's degree in anthropology. In 1969, she met Louis Leakey. She spoke to him about her dream of setting up a study on wild orangutans. Although he took some persuading, Louis was eventually convinced of Birutė's passion, and raised funds for a study, as he had done for Jane and Dian.

In 1971, Birutė arrived in Borneo, an island in Asia, to set up a research camp, named Camp Leakey after her mentor. It took a week of trekking through thick jungle to even spot an orangutan—then another twelve years to gain their trust. Today, with several prestigious awards under her belt, Birutė trains palm oil workers to respect and protect orangutans and their habitat. Thanks to her patience and dedication, we now know:

- Unlike chimpanzees and gorillas, orangutans do not live in big groups and are often solitary animals.
- Orangutans use tools; they have been observed modifying branches to become back scratchers or fly swatters.
- Orangutans have the longest birth interval (the time between each pregnancy) of any mammal. On average, orangutans give birth once every eight years.

⇃ THREE DEATHS ⇂

In the summer of 1968, Jane's favorite chimp, David Greybeard, was presumed to have died. He had gone missing several months before, and by July there was still no sign of him. Jane was heartbroken—they had shared a special bond. She later said, "When David disappeared, I mourned for him as I have no other chimpanzee before or since."

Then, in August 1972, Flo, another old friend, was found dead. To Jane's sadness, Flint, Flo's son, never recovered from her death. He became increasingly depressed and isolated, and died around three weeks later. Jane was convinced that he had died of grief. To honor Flo, Jane wrote an obituary that appeared in the *Sunday Times* newspaper in England. It was the first time that there had been an obituary to an animal in the paper. Jane talked about how much she and science had learned from Flo, but she also wrote:

But even if no one had studied the chimpanzees at Gombe, Flo's life, rich and full of vigor and love, would still have had a meaning and a significance in the patterns of things.

⋛ NEW LOVE ⋚

After her marriage ended, Jane put all of her energy
back into her work. She was busier than ever. Both
she and Hugo married again. Jane's second husband
was an Englishman named Derek Bryceson. Although
the two were often apart, friends considered Derek
to be the love of Jane's life.

When they met, Derek had just been appointed director of Tanzania's national parks, and was also a member of the government. Born in China in 1922, he had served as a fighter pilot in the British Royal Air Force during World War II. After only a few months, and at the age of just nineteen, he was shot down and left with a severely injured spine. Although doctors told him that he would never walk again, Derek was determined to prove them wrong. He taught himself to walk with the help of a cane, and with incredible amounts of willpower.

As director, Derek visited the parks regularly, flying in a small, four-seater Cessna plane. Sometimes Jane and Grub joined him for the ride, sitting behind Derek and the pilot. On one trip, they noticed a little plume of smoke coming from the instrument panel. They were flying over rugged, rocky land at the time, with nowhere to land until they reached Ruaha National Park, some forty-five minutes away. Keeping a close eye on the smoke, they finally reached Ruaha, and the pilot prepared to land. Just then, a herd of zebras decided to cross the runway, and the pilot pulled the plane up again.

But instead of
circling and coming
back to the runway,
the pilot tried to land
among the trees on the
far side of the river. The

plane slammed into the ground. One wing smashed a
tree, swinging the plane around. It continued to crash
through the bush, out of control, before coming to a
halt. Miraculously, everyone managed to get out of
the plane alive and unhurt, although they still had to
cross a crocodile-infested river to reach the safety
of the park's headquarters.

Jane knew that she had had a lucky escape—she
had been sure that she was about to die. The crash
showed her just how precious each moment of life can
be. When Derek asked her to marry him, she said yes
at once. They were married in 1975. Jane continued
to live in Gombe, overseeing the
research center. Derek stayed in
a house in Dar es Salaam, but
traveled to Gombe as often
as his work allowed.

⋛ THE FOUR-YEAR WAR ⋛

During her time at Gombe, Jane had come to believe that chimpanzees were very much like humans in many ways, only "rather nicer." However, the longer Jane observed the chimps, the more she realized that some of her early ideas were wrong. Just like humans, chimps have a very dark side.

For years, the chimps at Gombe had lived together as one united community. But over time, Jane began to notice divisions, and by 1972, the community has split into two separate groups. One group—the Kahama group—stayed in the south of the park; the other—the Kasakela group—stayed in the north. The smaller Kahama group was made up of six adult males, a juvenile male, as well as three adult females and their babies. The larger and more powerful Kasakela group was made up of eight adult males, twelve females, and their young.

Relations between the two groups were strained. The first serious outbreak of violence happened in January 1974. Six Kasakela males viciously attacked a Kahama adult male who had been feeding peacefully on his own. He died of his wounds soon afterward. Over the next four years, the Kasakela chimps killed the remaining Kahama adult males.

The Kahama adult females were also attacked. One was killed, and two went missing. By 1974, the whole Kahama group was wiped out, apart from three young females who became part of the Kasakela community.

The so-called Four-Year War shocked Jane to the core, and she struggled to come to terms with what she had seen. It changed her view of chimpanzee behavior forever. Far from being more peaceful, she now realized, chimps were as capable as humans of brutal and violent behavior toward each other.

KIDNAPPING AT GOMBE

While the chimps were waging war, human violence also reared its ugly head. By 1975, there were around twenty foreign students living and working at Gombe. They came from all over the world in search of a unique and enlightening experience. One night in May, their peaceful existence was suddenly, and terrifyingly, shattered. Forty armed men crossed Lake Tanganyika from Zaire (now the Democratic Republic of Congo) in a small boat and raided the camp. The men kidnapped four students—three American and one Dutch— tied them up, and took them back across the lake. Jane didn't hear about the raid until after the men had left. She gathered everyone together to try to work out what to do about the missing students.

It was very frightening. We didn't know where they had gone for quite a long time. We didn't even know if they were alive.

The next few weeks were very difficult for everyone, as they anxiously waited for news. The government ordered all foreigners to leave Gombe, so Jane, Grub, and many of the students moved to Dar es Salaam to stay in Derek's house. Eventually, after weeks of secret negotiations, a ransom was paid to the kidnappers, and the students were released unharmed. But Gombe was declared a "sensitive" area, and visitors, including Jane, needed government permission to come back. Foreign students were not allowed to live at Gombe again for several years. Instead, trained field staff from Tanzania took over the work.

GOMBE STREAM GAME RESERVE

Strictly NO ENTRY

Government authorized personnel only.

After the kidnappings, the future of the research center at Gombe looked bleak. With no students, it was difficult to ask organizations for money for research and for day-to-day running costs. Two of Jane's closest friends, Prince Ranieri di San Faustino and his wife, Genevieve, stepped in. In 1976, they helped to set up the Jane Goodall Institute in California. Through the work of the institute, Jane could now raise her own funds to keep the center going, ensuring the future of Gombe and her beloved chimps. At this turbulent time, Grub went to live with Vanne at the Birches, so that he could go to boarding school in England. Jane missed him dreadfully, but looked forward to the school breaks when Grub came back to Tanzania.

CHAPTER 6

RESCUE MISSION

In 1980, a very personal tragedy struck Jane's life. Derek began to suffer from stomach pains, and doctors in Dar es Salaam found a mass in his abdomen. Within a week, Jane and Derek were flying to England to get a second opinion from one of the top surgeons in the country. The doctor confirmed that Derek had a tumor in his colon, but that he could operate to remove it. He was hopeful that Derek would make a full recovery—it was the best news that they could have hoped for. But their happiness did not last long.

The operation showed that the cancer had spread throughout Derek's body, and he probably had only a few months to live. He died on October 12 of that year, in London, with Jane by his side. It was one of the darkest times of her life. Back in Tanzania, Jane held a memorial service for Derek, then scattered his ashes in the Indian Ocean, which he loved. A week later, she returned to Gombe, hoping that being back among the chimps would help her to cope with her grief.

⋛ CHIMPANZOO ⋚

To honor Derek's memory, Jane set up a new project called the ChimpanZoo. Shocked at the poor living conditions of the chimps she saw in zoos, she wanted to do something to help. Backed by the Jane Goodall Institute, Ann Pierce, a former student from Gombe, set off to visit various zoos in the United States, collecting information about the behavior of about 130 chimps. Combining this data with knowledge of how chimps behave in the wild, ChimpanZoo began to campaign for larger enclosures for captive chimps, and homes that are more like their wild habitat

Founded in 1984, ChimpanZoo is still thriving today. Trained students and volunteers visit zoos, observing how the chimps behave and comparing this behavior to that of chimps in the wild. The results help zoos to improve the conditions in which they keep their chimps, and to find ways of enriching the chimps' lives.

⋛ LIFE-CHANGING EVENT ⋚

Back in Gombe, Jane was kept busy overseeing the work of the research center. The ban on visitors and students had been lifted, and the place buzzed once more with activity. In the middle of this, Jane embarked on a long and draining project, writing a book called *The Chimpanzees of Gombe*. The book drew on years' and years' worth of research that Jane had stored in boxes and filing cabinets in her house in Dar es Salaam. Sifting through it all was a monumental task, even with the help of several research assistants. Incredibly, by 1983, the book was almost finished. With nineteen chapters and hundreds of photographs, it was the most thorough work on chimpanzee behavior ever written. It was finally published, to great acclaim, in 1986, and remains a must-have book for many primatologists.

The Chimpanzees of Gombe
Patterns of Behavior   Jane Goodall

To celebrate the publication of the book, a three-day conference was held in November 1986 in Chicago. Called "Understanding Chimpanzees," it attracted chimpanzee experts from around the world. They began by discussing their research, but later moved on to a more alarming subject—the uncertain future of chimps in the wild. Across Africa, wild chimps were in serious danger of becoming extinct, unless urgent steps were taken. A century earlier, there had been around a million chimps; at the time of the conference, there were as few as 200,000. People were clearing the chimps' forest home for timber, and to make space for villages, farms, and mines.

They also hunted chimps for their meat (known as bushmeat), which they sold as a delicacy for large sums of money. Some people sold parts of chimps, such as their hands and feet, as novelty items, or ground those parts up into supposedly magical potions. They also caught baby chimps and sold them to the pet trade, entertainment industry, zoos, or for medical experiments. They killed the mothers, then snatched the traumatized babies.

Dian's Death

A terrible event that had occurred a year before the "Understanding Chimpanzees" conference brought home just how dangerous the poaching trade could be—for all primates. Dian Fossey, one of Louis's prodigal primatologists, had been brutally murdered while studying gorillas in Rwanda, Africa. The authorities suspected poachers were behind the attack. Jane was horrified by Dian's death. Though she had found Dian "very difficult, very opinionated," she admired her for having brought gorillas to the world's attention. It was another reminder that Jane's field of study was full of very real risks.

At the end of the conference, the delegates decided to form an organization to help save wild chimps, and lobby for better care and living conditions for those in captivity. The new group was called the Committee for the Conservation and Care of Chimpanzees (CCCC). To Jane's delight, it was headed by Ann Pierce. For Jane, the conference would prove life changing. For twenty-five years, she had lived her dream of observing chimps in the wild. Now, it was time to use her celebrity status to fight for their rights and future, not just in Gombe, but all over the world.

When I arrived in Chicago, I was a research scientist, planning the second volume of *The Chimpanzees of Gombe*. When I left, I was already, in my heart, committed to conservation and education.

For years, Jane had concentrated her efforts solely on the chimps at Gombe and had shown little interest in the plight of chimps elsewhere. She later admitted that she had kept herself to her own little world. She knew that the forest around Gombe was disappearing, but so far, the chimps she observed were safe. The conference changed all that. Jane heard about the terrible plight of primates in other parts of the world. Apes, and their habitats, were vanishing fast—urgent action needed to be taken before it was too late. For years, Jane had lived her dream life with the chimps at Gombe. Now, the conference had opened her eyes.

PROTECT THE CHIMPS!

NO POACHING

SAVE THE RAIN FOREST!

She traveled to different countries in Africa with an exhibit called "Understanding Chimpanzees." She met presidents, government officials, and conservationists involved in chimpanzee research. She visited schools, gave lectures, and made media appearances, campaigning tirelessly to highlight the plight of chimps, and the need to protect them.

In the United States, Jane worked closely with the CCCC, which was pushing for zoos and labs to be more aware of the physical and mental health of the chimps in their care. She lobbied the government in Washington, DC, and appeared on many television shows. Soon, the work was taking her away from Gombe for longer and longer periods, and she was able to get there only a few times a year. It was a strain, but Jane knew that she was doing the right thing.

Chimpanzees used to live in twenty-five countries across Africa, in an area almost the size of the United States. Today, chimps are endangered in five of those countries and extinct in five others.

<u>Chimps in Trouble</u>

Status: Endangered (IUCN* Red List)

Numbers in

the wild: c. 175,000–300,000

Habitat: Forests

Main threats: • Habitat destruction

                       • Poaching for bushmeat

                       • Capture for pet trade

                       • Exposure to disease

*International Union for Conservation of Nature

⧝ A SHOCKING VISIT ⧜

In 1987, Jane faced one of her most grueling
challenges yet. While spending Christmas with her
family at the Birches, she received a videotape. It
had been secretly filmed by animal rights activists
inside a large medical research laboratory—SEMA,
Inc.—in the United States. The lab housed around five
hundred primates, including chimps, that were used to
test vaccines for human diseases, such as AIDS. The
animals were monitored to see if the vaccine worked
or not. Many died slow and painful deaths.

Jane and her family watched the video in horror—too shocked, angry, and sad to speak. The tape showed young chimps kept in tiny cages with barely enough room to move. They were clearly suffering from depression—it was a horrific scene.

Jane had known that chimps were used in medical research, but had no idea that things were so bleak. But, before she could speak out against the cruelty, she needed to see conditions for herself. To her surprise, she was given permission to visit the SEMA lab. The experience was more disturbing than she could possibly have dreamed. She saw chimps kept in isolation, in steel boxes with tiny windows, and chimps whose eyes were dull and blank, with no hope. For animals used to friendly contact, family ties, and fun, it was unbearable.

Would you put a human child in a small cage alone with no companionship?

After SEMA, Jane toured other labs and research facilities around the world. She spoke out about what she saw, urging governments and officials to improve conditions for the animals based on their natural behavior and lifestyle. Her hope was that, one day, scientists would no longer use animals for testing medicines. "But until that happens," she wrote, "it is desperately urgent that we try to give those animals being used today much better places to live, much better care, much more respect, and much more love."

CHIMPS IN REHAB

On Jane's travels around Africa, she often came across individual chimps that she tried to help. Many were orphans whose mothers had been shot for meat or so that hunters could steal their babies for the live animal trade. One day, Jane came across a baby chimpanzee for sale in a tourist market in Zaire. He had a piece of string tied tightly around his waist, and this was attached to the top of a tiny wire cage. When Jane spotted him, he was curled up on his side, and his eyes were dull and lifeless. It would not be long before he was dead. Heartbroken, Jane made the tiny panting sound that chimps use to greet each other. To her amazement, the chimpanzee sat up, looked at her, and reached out to touch her face.

Jane did not know what to do. If she bought him, the hunters would only try to get more babies to sell. But she couldn't just leave him.

She went to see the American ambassador, who contacted the minister of the environment. It was illegal to sell chimps without a license, but nobody took any notice of this law. The minister agreed to help, and called the police, who confiscated the baby chimp. Jane cut the rope with a knife—he was free. But he was very sick and frightened, and could not be released back into the wild. A friend, Graziella Cotman, agreed to help nurse "Little Jay" back to health. He was the first of many orphans that Jane and her organization would help.

In 1992, the government of the Congo, together with the Jane Goodall Institute, created the Tchimpounga Chimpanzee Rehabilitation Center in a protected patch of forest. It provides a sanctuary for orphaned and rescued chimps who can never be released back into the wild. Staff members nurse the chimps back to health, introduce them to other chimps, and help them to feel and behave like chimps again. Today, the center is home to around 160 chimps who live in natural, but protected, conditions.

⋛ TCHIMPOUNGA CHIMPS ⋛

Name: Rickie

Animal: Chimpanzee

Rescued: 1990s

Life story:
- Stolen to be sold as a pet
- Best friend was Henri, a shaggy dog

Name: Gregoire

Animal: Chimpanzee

Rescued: 1997

Life story:
- Spent forty-six years in a zoo in the Congo
- Taught to dance for bananas

Name: Wounda
Animal: Chimpanzee
Rescued: 2014
Life story: • Rescued from the bushmeat
               trade
             • Given the first chimp-to-
               chimp blood transfusion
               in Africa

Name: Kabi
Animal: Chimpanzee
Rescued: 2018
Life story: • Saw his whole family
               butchered
             • Received life-saving,
               24-hour care

The 1980s had begun with personal tragedy for Jane, when her greatly loved husband Derek died. She had been afraid that the research center would have to close down. It had taken Gombe and its extraordinary magic to help her cope with her grief and get back on her feet again. By the end of the decade, Jane's life had changed dramatically. Her book, *The Chimpanzees of Gombe*, had brought her public acknowledgment and given her the confidence she needed. She was now totally committed to a new cause—the welfare of all animals, in Africa and beyond. It was time for Jane to take her place on the world stage. She was determined to face any challenges thrown her way head-on.

CHAPTER 7

CAMPAIGNING FOR CHANGE

From the mid-1980s, Jane traveled tirelessly around the
world, rarely spending very long in one place. She gave
lectures, visited zoos and wildlife parks, and met thousands
of adoring fans. Her aim was, and still is, to raise awareness
of the plight of chimps and other endangered animals, and
to try to safeguard a better future for the world. When
people ask her why she works so hard and travels so much,
she replies simply, "I owe it to the chimps."

⋛ GOMBE MOVES ON ⋚

Jane was now spending so much time on the move
that she was only able to snatch short visits to Gombe
in between her other engagements. Although she
missed the forest and the chimps very much, she knew
that she had left them in good hands. In her absence,
the students made many exciting discoveries, and the
research center went from strength to strength.

One discovery began with a tragedy. In 1987, an
outbreak of pneumonia killed eleven chimps. Among
them was the mother of a three-year-old male
chimp called Mel. Lost and alone, Mel grew weak and
sickly. It seemed quite likely that he would die. To
the researchers' astonishment, a young male chimp
named Spindle took over Mel's care. Spindle shared
his food with Mel, carried Mel on his back when they
went on long trips, and even let Mel sleep in his nest
at night. Spindle protected Mel from the other chimps
and taught him the survival skills he needed.

This was the first known example of a male chimp
looking after another chimp, even though the two
were not related. It showed that chimps are capable of
showing concern for the well-being of others.

⋚ ROOTS & SHOOTS ⋚

Very early on in her campaign, Jane realized how important it was to get young people involved in conservation. As well as writing children's books, she began giving talks in local schools in Tanzania. Everywhere she visited, the children were fascinated by animals and determined to protect their environment. In 1991, Jane invited a group of twelve local schoolchildren to her house in Dar es Salaam. They sat on Jane's front porch and chatted about the challenges facing their local areas, and discussed what could be done. They told Jane that they'd like to learn more, but that their schools didn't cover topics such as animal welfare or the environment, nor did they have any resources that could help them.

Jane encouraged them to go back to their schools and form groups to take action. This new program became known as "Roots & Shoots," because roots form a firm foundation underground, and shoots grow upward with great strength. The aim was for the groups to take on small-scale projects that would benefit their local communities. For example, the original twelve members tried to get local fishermen to stop using harmful dynamite to flush out fish.

To Jane's delight, the program was an instant success and grew very quickly. Today, there are thousands of Roots & Shoots groups in more than 140 countries, with some 150,000 members. There is a newsletter and annual conference so that members can come together and exchange ideas, and also awards for groups and individuals. Current projects include tackling the problem of the millions of wooden chopsticks thrown away every day, clearing trash from mountains, reducing the carbon footprint of schools, and planting crops to stop baboons from raiding farmers' fields.

The best way to create the kind of change that we need . . . is for everybody to spend just a few minutes each day thinking about the consequences of the choices they make.

⋛ COMMUNITY CONSERVATION ⋛

Another exciting project began in 1994, when Jane set up Lake Tanganyika Catchment Reforestation and Education (TACARE). At that time, the forest around Kigoma was being cut down at an alarming rate. As the forest and its resources of materials and food disappeared, chimps and other wildlife were losing their homes, and local people also faced losing their main source of food.

Many of the people living around Kigoma were very poor. They struggled to find enough food for their families and to make a living. Jane realized that they were far more likely to help protect wildlife if their own lives could be improved. It was vital to make them feel involved in any conservation work. By offering small loans of money, TACARE helped villagers to set up nurseries where they could grow trees to replace those that had been cut down. The project worked well, and soon there were nurseries all along the lake. The new trees helped to bring the forests back to life. Today, villagers are trained by TACARE to patrol the forests using smartphones and tablets to record every time they see a tree that has been illegally cut down.

"When you live in the forest, it's easy to see that everything's connected."
—Jane Goodall

STRATEGIES FOR CHANGE

The Jane Goodall Institute has nine key strategies that work together to bring community-centered conservation to life:

1. CONSERVATION SCIENCE
Using the latest, cutting-edge science and technology, such as satellites and UAV remote sensing (using drones to take photographs), to monitor species and habitats.

2. ADVOCACY
Speaking out on behalf of local people, animals, and the environment to try to get laws and policies changed.

3. PUBLIC AWARENESS
Helping local people understand the laws protecting species such as chimps. Teaching children to respect the environment they live in.

4. HEALTHY HABITATS
Working with governments and local communities to protect habitats and keep them healthy for everyone.

5. GENDER AND HEALTH
Helping young women to get better education and health care, and have a greater say in their futures.

6. SUSTAINABLE LIVELIHOODS
Working with local people to find alternative sources of income that don't harm the environment and its natural resources.

7. PROTECTING GREAT APES
Saving chimps and other great apes through laws, education programs, and the setting up of sanctuaries.

8. ROOTS & SHOOTS
Encouraging young people to identify problems in their communities, and work toward finding a solution.

9. RESEARCH
Learning more about wild chimps and other primates through the groundbreaking work at Gombe. Training primate researchers and scientists.

[Courtesy: The Jane Goodall Institute]

⋛ MEETING MR. H ⋚

Jane always travels with a very special stuffed toy monkey called "Mr. H." A friend named Gary Haun gave him to Jane as a birthday gift in 1996. Gary had lost his eyesight in a helicopter crash when he was twenty-one years old, but was determined to become a magician. People told him that this was impossible, but that didn't put him off. He never gave up, and he proved everyone wrong—he has also skydived, swum with sharks, and climbed Kilimanjaro, Africa's highest mountain. Gary actually thought that he had given Jane a chimpanzee, but Jane showed him that the toy had a tail (chimps and other apes don't have tails). But that didn't stop Jane from adopting Mr. H as her mascot and taking him with her wherever she goes. To Jane, Mr. H stands for hope and is a symbol of Gary's incredible spirit and strength.

> Mr. H has visited more than sixty countries with Jane, and met millions of adoring fans.

Despite her exhausting schedule, Jane still makes as much time as possible for her family, and stays at the Birches, her old home, whenever she is in England. Her sister, Judy, now lives there with her family, and Jane's first toy chimpanzee, Jubilee, still sits on her old bed. Jane is also close to her son, Grub, who is married with two children, Merlin and Angel. Grub lives in Dar es Salaam, next to Jane's own house, and works as a boatbuilder. Although Grub is still not keen on chimps, his son shares Jane's passion for animals and the natural world.

Hugo, Jane's first husband, sadly died from cancer in 2000. Then a year later, Jane's beloved mother, Vanne, died. She had been Jane's traveling companion and greatest supporter, always encouraging her to follow her dreams. Without Vanne, Jane says, she might never have gone to Africa.

Jane's Books

Over the past fifty years, Jane has written hundreds of articles and several books. Many are about the Gombe chimps; others are about Jane's life and her hopes for the planet's future. Among these books are many for young readers—here is a selection:

- *Grub, the Bush Baby* (1972)
  The story of Jane's family life in Africa, and especially the adventures of her son, Grub.

- *My Life with the Chimpanzees* (1988)
  Jane's story of how she went to Africa, and became the world's leading expert on chimpanzees.

- *With Love* (1994)
  Ten stories about the Gombe chimpanzees, showing their care and compassion.

- *The Chimpanzees I Love: Saving Their World and Ours* (2001)
  Jane's account of her life among the chimpanzees at Gombe, with a message of hope for the future.

≡ HAPPY BIRTHDAY, DR. JANE! ≡

On April 3, 2014, Jane turned eighty years old. The Wildlife Conservation Network (WCN) held a birthday party in her honor in San Francisco. Jane had been a great supporter of the WCN's work for many years. The original idea was for a fairly small-scale event, with food and drink served by WCN volunteers. But Jane had a very special birthday wish.

She wanted to move one hundred rescued chimps from the center at Tchimpounga to three islands in the nearby river, where they could live as they would in the wild, but with care if they needed it. With one hundred times more forest to roam, the chimps would enjoy much more freedom in the new area. It would also make space for more chimps at Tchimpounga, which was fast running out of room.

Of course, this would cost money. So the plans for Jane's party changed. It turned into a lavish evening with dinner, music, and an auction. The auction raised more than $1.25 million for the chimps. At the end of the night, Jane thanked everyone for celebrating with her and for making her wish come true.

So far, about sixty of the strongest chimps have relocated. Among them is Wounda (see page 107), who was rescued from the bushmeat trade and arrived at Tchimpounga in a pitiful state. With around-the-clock care from staff and vets, she made an incredible recovery and was eventually ready for the move. A video of Wounda's release was seen around the world. As she gets out of her traveling

crate, she turns and gives Jane, whom she has never met before, a massive hug. Jane said that this was one of the most moving experiences of her life, and the best birthday present ever.

⋛ BACK TO GOMBE ⋜

It has been almost sixty years since Jane first arrived at Gombe to begin her life's work with the chimps. Over the years, Gombe itself has faced many threats. By the end of the last century, it had been reduced to a small patch of forest, and the chimps had begun to disappear. But the research center is still going, conducting the longest-running study of wild chimpanzee behavior in the world. Most of the research is done by Tanzanians from local villages, but experts still come from around the world, thrilled to be able to track the chimpanzees. Trackers set off early for the chimps' nesting sites and wait for them to wake up. After that, they follow the chimps, from a safe distance, as they move about during the day. The chimps might stay in one small patch of forest, or roam for many miles, up- and downhill, and through tangled plants and vines. Chimp tracking can be tough and painful, but it's mostly lots of fun!

In 2018, the United Nations Educational, Scientific, and Cultural Organization (UNESCO) recognized Gombe as an official biosphere reserve, adding to over 400 biospheres already in existence around the world. These are places where communities live in harmony with the natural world that surrounds them. On hearing this, Jane said, "It is wonderful news. I hope that it will lead to more recognition of a truly unique area that is home to almost all of Tanzania's remaining chimpanzee population, as well as for many other animals and their habitats."

We could change the world tomorrow, if all the millions of people around the world acted the way they believe.

CONCLUSION

A BETTER WORLD

Almost sixty years after arriving at Gombe, Jane is now recognized as the world's leading expert in chimpanzees. Her work changed the whole face of primate research, revolutionized our understanding of chimps, and altered the way in which scientists recognize the links between humans and apes. She has helped to improve life for chimps in zoos and in medical laboratories, and the Jane Goodall Institute has helped to fund hundreds of people and projects, including several other chimp research centers in Africa.

Now in her eighties, Jane still travels approximately three hundred days a year, inspiring sell-out audiences at her lectures and talks. Her fans admire her wisdom, modesty, and courage in taking on such a huge challenge. She's also appeared in numerous documentaries and television programs. In 2019, she was featured in a British television series called *Icons*. The aim of the series was to find the greatest person of the twentieth century, and the icons were picked by experts based on their achievements, impact, and legacy.

⋍ CHIMPANZEE PIONEER ⋍

Before Jane began her work at Gombe, scientists did not know that chimps:

→ make and use tools
→ eat meat as well as plants
→ have complex societies
→ have distinct personalities
→ wage war on each other

Jane's trailblazing discoveries changed all that. She showed people that science is all about getting involved—both physically and emotionally—rather than wearing a white coat and spending hours in a lab. Today, it's common practice to name animals in scientific studies and take a more hands-on approach to interacting with wild animals.

"They should have names. They're individuals. And that's been my fight from the beginning—every animal has an individuality, just like every human being. And without a name, the individuality kind of fizzles away."
—Jane Goodall

It's easy to forget how difficult the work was for Jane. For most of the time, she was on her own, in challenging terrain, and among animals that could easily turn dangerous. On many occasions, her life and health were at risk. Dian Fossey's story proved that being out in the field could be life-threatening. Jane had no technology to help or protect her, but set off into the forest each day, armed only with her trusty binoculars, notebook, pen, lunch, and astonishing amounts of patience and determination. For Jane, the most important thing was to respect the chimps she was privileged to observe. After all, she said, the chimps belonged in the forest, and she and her students did not.

⋝ CHIMPFACE ⋜

Unlike Jane, today's conservationists have a range of sophisticated technology at their fingertips. This includes laptop computers for recording data, and satellites and computer software for mapping and monitoring wildlife populations. Technology can be used to track down poachers and identify habitats under threat. For example, rangers place cell phones in some forests; the phones detect the noise of chainsaws and send notifications to the rangers to warn them of illegal logging.

One of the most exciting new technologies is called ChimpFace. It is helping to tackle the illegal trade in chimpanzees. It uses software to search social media sites for the faces of chimps being offered for sale. The software then compares these faces with photos held on a database. If there is a match, the authorities can track down the owner of the social media account and take action.

In the future, the team at Gombe hopes to use ChimpFace to track individual chimps and groups, and monitor their health.

⋛ CLEVER CHIMPS ⋚

As Jane discovered, chimps are extremely intelligent animals. They can solve problems, plan ahead, and are fast learners. In 1966, two American psychologists, Allen and Beatrix Gardner, adopted a ten-month-old female chimp named Washoe. Born in Africa, she was captured and sold to the US Air Force for use in medical tests as part of the space program.

Chimps communicate with each other using gestures, facial expressions, hoots, grunts, and pants. But they do not have the right voice box to produce language like humans. The Gardners taught Washoe to communicate with them using American Sign Language. By the end of the experiment, Washoe knew more than three hundred signs. One day, she even made the signs for water and bird when she saw a picture of a swan.

≡ HAPPY WORLD CHIMPANZEE DAY! ≡

The first World Chimpanzee Day was held on July 14, 2018, and is set to become an annual event. It aims to celebrate all things chimpanzee, and to raise awareness of the threats facing chimps today. More than sixty zoos and organizations around the world took part, including the Jane Goodall Institute.

It held an art competition to find the best picture featuring a chimpanzee, and also encouraged people to become Chimpanzee Guardians to help save orphaned chimps from illegal hunting. The date of July 14 was chosen because on that day in 1960, Jane first set foot in Gombe. A baby chimp, born just after midnight on World Chimpanzee Day at Detroit Zoo, was named Jane in her honor.

"Put simply, chimpanzees are absolutely amazing animals! I am proud and humbled to state that I am 99 percent chimpanzee."
—Stuart Nixon,
Chester Zoo, England

HONORING JANE

Jane's trailblazing work has earned her hundreds of honors and awards from all around the world. In 2002, she was appointed a Messenger of Peace by the UN at a ceremony in New York. The UN praised her for her "devotion to the creation of a safer and more stable world, [and] the fostering of human rights and the liberation of the human spirit." In 2004, she traveled to Buckingham Palace in London, where Prince Charles made her a Dame of the British Empire. There is now a petition for Dame Jane to be given a Nobel Peace Prize.

MAJOR PRIZES AND AWARDS

1990 *Kyoto Prize*, Japan

1996 *The Tanzanian Kilimanjaro Medal*

2002 *UN Messenger of Peace*

2004 *Dame of the British Empire*

2006 *French Legion of Honor*;
UNESCO Gold Medal Award

2010 *International Golden Doves for
Peace Award*, **Italy**

In 1960, Jane Goodall was given an extraordinary opportunity to follow her dreams of working with wild animals in Africa. She grabbed the chance with both hands and has never looked back. Today, she continues to work tirelessly to try to change the world for not only her beloved chimpanzees, but for everyone. Her life and work are hugely inspiring, and she is a hero to many people. Jane is especially keen to encourage girls to become scientists, as she did almost sixty years ago.

⋛ PRIMATOLOGY PIONEERS ⋛

When Jane began her trailblazing work, primatology was mostly a man's world. Today, things have changed dramatically, and many of the world's leading primatologists are women. Along with Dian Fossey and Birutė Galdikas, Jane proved that women could be patient, meticulous, and professional. Today, over fifty percent of scientists working in the field are female.

But Jane is a great believer that every individual has a part to play in making the world a better place for all living things. Everyone can make a difference, even if they can only make small changes in their everyday lives, one action at a time. The power of these small actions put together gives Jane hope for the future, and her life and work are shining examples of what individuals can achieve if they put their minds to it.

Timeline

April 3
Jane Goodall is born.

September 1
World War II begins in Europe.

1934   1935   1939

February
Jubilee, the chimpanzee, is born at London Zoo, England.

Jane and her family move to Bournemouth, England.

July 14
Jane and her mother, Vanne, arrive at Gombe Stream Game Reserve.

March 28
Jane marries Hugo van Lawick.

1960   1964

November 4
Jane observes chimps using tools to eat termites. Later that year, she observes chimps eating meat.

Two African states, Tanganyika and Zanzibar, merge to form the United Republic of Tanzania.

September 2
World War II
ends.

March 13
Jane travels
to Africa
for the
first time.

1945   1948   1957

Apartheid
begins in
South Africa.

Jane receives
her PhD from
Cambridge
University in
England.

March
Jane and
Hugo have
a son,
whom they
nickname
"Grub."

1965   1967   1968

The Gombe
Stream
Research
Center is
founded.

Jane's
favorite
chimpanzee,
David Greybeard,
goes missing.

Jane's first book, *In the Shadow of Man*, is published.

The Four-Year War begins.

Jane marries Derek Bryceson.

1971   1974   1975

Jane and Hugo get divorced.

December 26 Dian Fossey is murdered in Rwanda.

Jane founds the Roots & Shoots organization.

1985   1986   1991

November Jane attends a conference about chimpanzees in Chicago and begins a campaign for conservation.

Derek dies
of cancer.

1977   1980   1984

Jane founds
the Jane
Goodall
Institute
(JGI).

The
ChimpanZoo
project
begins.

Apartheid
ends in
South
Africa.

1992   1993   1994

The Tchimpounga
Chimpanzee
Rehabilitation
Center is
established.

Jane launches
TACARE (The
Lake Tanganyika
Catchment
Reforestation
and Education
project).

August 2
The Second
Congo War/Great
War of Africa
begins.

July 18
The Second
Congo War ends,
with around
three to six
million deaths.

1998   2002   2003

April 16
Jane is
appointed
as a UN
Messenger
of Peace.

Gombe is
recognized as
an official
UNESCO biosphere
reserve.

2018

July 14
The first
World
Chimpanzee
Day is
celebrated.

Jane receives the French Legion of Honor and a UNESCO Gold Medal Award.

2004   2006   2014

February 20
Jane is made a Dame of the British Empire.

April 3
Jane celebrates her 80th birthday.

Further Reading

→ *In the Shadow of Man* by Jane Goodall
  (Mariner Books, 2010)

→ *Jane Goodall (DK Life Stories)* by Libby Romero
  (DK Children, 2019)

→ *My Life with the Chimpanzees* by Jane Goodall
  (Aladdin, revised edition, 1996)

→ *Untamed: The Wild Life of Jane Goodall* by Anita
  Silvey (National Geographic Children's Books, 2015)

Websites

→ janegoodall.org

The website of the Jane Goodall Institute, a global conservation organization that promotes Jane's vision and work.

→ rootsandshoots.org

Jane's organization for young people who want to change their local environments. There are now branches all around the world.

Glossary

air raid: An attack by aircraft.

aluminum: A lightweight, silvery-gray metal.

botanist: A scientist who studies plants.

carbon footprint: The amount of carbon dioxide released into the atmosphere by the activities of a person, organization, or community.

colon: The main part of the large intestine.

conservationists: People who work to protect wildlife and the environment.

DNA: Deoxyribonucleic acid. The material that carries information about how a living thing looks and functions.

documentary: A film or television program featuring real people and real events.

Glossary

epidemic: A widespread outbreak of a disease in a community at a particular time.

evolution: The process by which living things can gradually change over time.

herbivores: Animals that feed on plants.

naturalist: A person who studies or is an expert in nature.

obituary: A notice of a death, often in a newspaper, that includes a short biography of the person's life.

omnivores: Animals that eat both plants and animals.

parasite: An organism that lives on or in another living thing and gets nourishment from it, at the host's expense.

physiotherapy: The treatment of injuries and illnesses by using massage and exercise.

<u>Glossary</u>

ransom: A sum of money demanded or paid for the release of a captive.

rationing: A fixed amount of food that a person is allowed during times of shortage, such as war.

refugees: People who are forced to leave their countries to escape from war, natural disasters, or persecution.

termite: A tiny ant-like insect.

thesis: A long essay written by a student to gain a university degree.

tsetse fly: An African fly that bites people and other mammals and sucks their blood, spreading diseases such as sleeping sickness.

Glossary

tumor: A lump or swelling in a part of the body.

vaccine: A medicine given to protect people and animals from disease.

zoology: The scientific study of animals.

Index

Index

Index

Index

Mange, Marie Claude "Clo,"
34, 39, 40

Mel (chimpanzee), 120

Mike (chimpanzee), 66

monkeys, 8, 9, 52, 54, 58

Morris-Goodall, Judith (Judy),
11, 16, 21, 26, 72–73, 129

Morris-Goodall, Mortimer,
11, 16, 26

Morris-Goodall, Vanne, 11, 13,
14, 15, 16, 19, 26, 30, 36,
48–49, 50, 51, 53, 56, 64,
85, 100, 129

Mr. H (toy), 128

Mr. McGregor (chimpanzee),
64, 65, 79

N

National Geographic Society,
63, 72–73, 75, 77

naturalist, 14

Nissen, Henry W., 47

Nutt, Mrs. "Danny Nutt," 14, 16

O

Olly (aunt), 31, 32

orangutans, 54, 84, 88–89

Oxford University, 32–33

P

paleoanthropologist, 41

Pierce, Ann, 102, 106

pneumonia, 120

polio, 31, 79

primatology, 8–9, 54, 103,
105, 135, 144

psychology, 88

R

Roots & Shoots program,
122–123

Rusty (dog), 25

Rwanda, 86, 105

  Karisoke Research Center,
  86

S

San Faustino, Prince Ranieri di
and Genevieve, 100

SEMA, Inc., 110

Serengeti, 82

South Africa, 37, 38

Spindle (chimpanzee), 120

Swahili (language) 64, 80

<u>Index</u>

FOLLOW THE TRAIL!

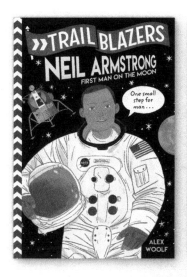

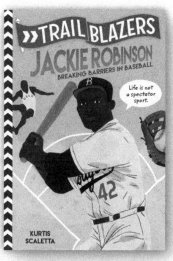

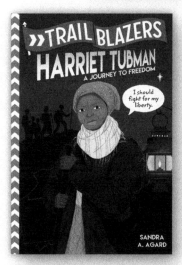

TURN THE PAGE FOR A SNEAK PEEK AT THESE TRAILBLAZERS BIOGRAPHIES!

Excerpt text copyright © 2019 by Alex Woolf.
Excerpt illustrations copyright © 2019 by Artful Doodlers.
Published in the United States by Random House Children's Books,
a division of Penguin Random House LLC, New York.

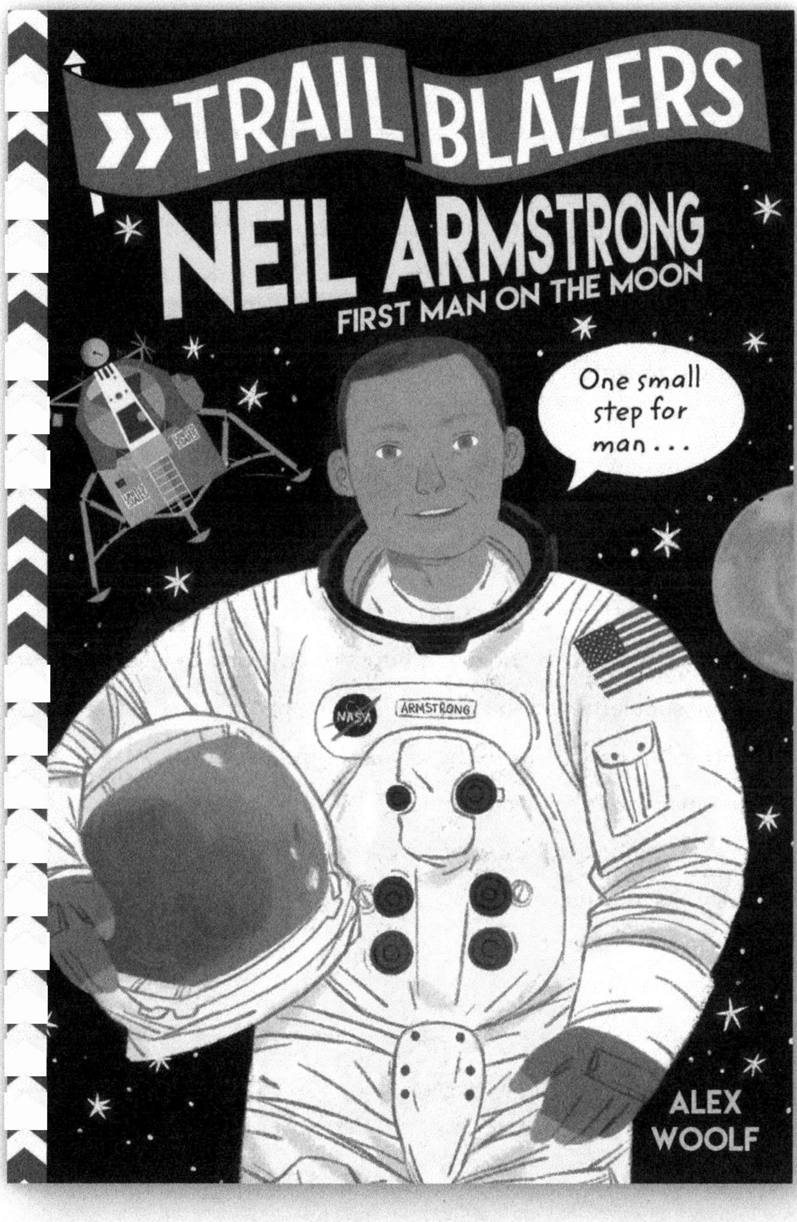
TRAIL BLAZERS
NEIL ARMSTRONG
FIRST MAN ON THE MOON
One small step for man . . .
ARMSTRONG
NASA
ALEX WOOLF

⋛ FLYING LESSONS ⋛

Airplanes remained Neil's first love. His dream was to become both a pilot and an aeronautical engineer—someone who designs and builds planes. About three or four miles outside Wapakoneta was Port Koneta Airport. Neil cycled or hitchhiked there as often as he could to watch the planes land and take off, and talk to the pilots.

When he was fifteen, Neil began saving up for flying lessons. He got a job at Rhine and Brading's Pharmacy, where he earned forty cents an hour. A one-hour flying lesson cost nine dollars, so he had to work twenty-two and a half hours to pay for one lesson! Neil supplemented his earnings at the pharmacy by offering to wash down the airplanes at Port Koneta. He even helped the airport mechanics with some routine maintenance work, servicing the planes' cylinders, pistons, and valves.

Eventually, Neil had saved up enough money to pay for some lessons. A veteran army pilot named Aubrey Knudegard taught him. They flew in a light, high-wing monoplane called an Aeronca Champion.

Aircraft Fact File

Name:	Aeronca Champion
Nickname:	"Champ"
Length:	21.5 ft. (6.6 m)
Wingspan:	35.2 ft. (10.7 m)
Engine:	65 horsepower
Top speed:	100 mph (161 kmh)
First flight:	April 29, 1944

Project Gemini

The purpose of Project Gemini was to develop space-travel techniques that would be needed for the Apollo program, which aimed to land astronauts on the moon. Two of the critical techniques that needed to be developed were:

- extra-vehicular activity (EVA)— when astronauts leave the spacecraft in their spacesuits to work outside it

- space rendezvous and docking—when two spacecraft join together in orbit

BECOMING AN ASTRONAUT

Two months earlier, Mercury astronaut John Glenn had become the first American to orbit Earth. His achievement had captured the public imagination like nothing since Charles Lindbergh's famous transatlantic flight in 1927. Neil saw there was real excitement surrounding NASA's space program, and he wondered if he should be part of it. However, he delayed sending in his application and missed the June 1 deadline by about a week.

Luckily, a man named Dick Day was one of the people in charge of selecting the new astronauts. He had worked with Neil at Edwards, and he thought him better qualified than anyone to be an astronaut. When Neil's application came in, Day slipped it into the pile with all the other applications so no one would realize it was late. In September 1962, Neil was thrilled to learn that he had been selected as one of the new astronauts.

⋛ WALKING ON THE MOON ⋚

Buzz soon followed Neil out, and the two of them explored the lunar surface. "It has a stark beauty all its own," remarked Neil. Buzz described it as "magnificent desolation." The powdery soil was quite slippery, they discovered, but walking was no problem. They unveiled a commemorative plaque that had been mounted on *Eagle*'s base.

They planted a US flag, stiffened with wire to make it look like it was flying in a breeze. Neil photographed Buzz saluting it.

President Richard Nixon called them by radio-telephone from the White House. "This certainly has to be the most historic telephone call ever made," he said. "I just can't tell you how proud we all are of what you've done. . . . For one priceless moment in the whole history of man, all the people of this Earth are truly one."

Neil and Buzz spent the rest of the EVA collecting rock and soil samples and performing experiments. They set up devices to sense moonquakes and to measure the distance between the moon and Earth. Those devices would stay on the moon.

Excerpt text copyright © 2019 by Kurtis Scaletta.
Excerpt illustrations copyright © 2019 by Artful Doodlers.
Published in the United States by Random House Children's Books,
a division of Penguin Random House LLC, New York.

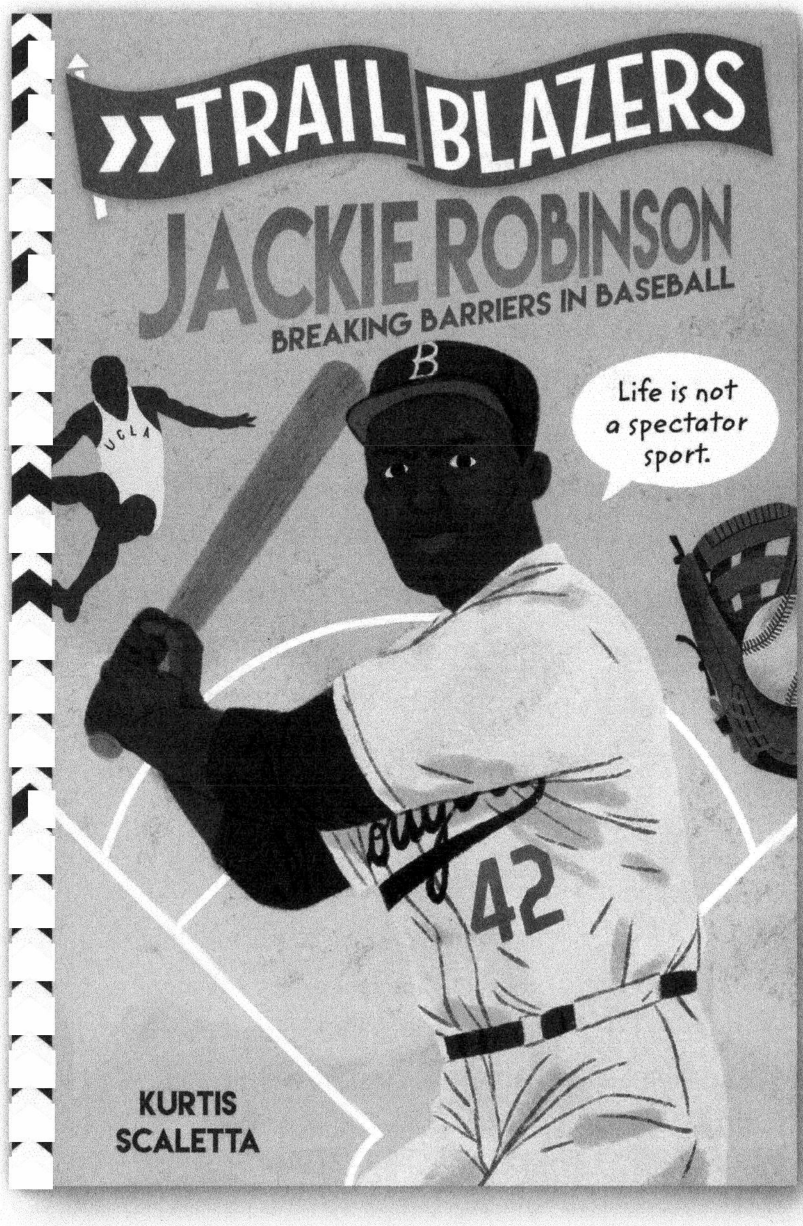
TRAIL BLAZERS
JACKIE ROBINSON
BREAKING BARRIERS IN BASEBALL
Life is not a spectator sport.
UCLA
B
42
KURTIS SCALETTA

Jackie at UCLA
1939-1941

→ **Football:** Jackie is called "the greatest ball carrier in the nation." In 1939, the Bruins go undefeated, though three games end in ties.

→ **Basketball:** Dazzling play by Jackie helps end a long losing streak by the Bruins but isn't enough to give them a winning season.

→ **Baseball:** Jackie once again plays short and gets a reputation for stealing bases but goes into a hitting slump he can't break out of.

→ **Track and Field:** Jackie sets a conference record and wins the NCAA title for the long jump.

→ **Combined:** Jackie is the first athlete at UCLA to "letter" in four sports—meaning he has significant playing time at the varsity level.

≥ LOVE AND WAR ≤

Jackie continued to shine in his second year at ULCA, but the football team and basketball team both had losing seasons. Something happened that was more important than sports or even his education. He met a student named Rachel Isum. Jackie was drawn to Rachel's intelligence and compassion.

At first, he later wrote, Jackie experienced a new kind of prejudice. Rachel Isum knew he was a star athlete and had seen him play. She was convinced he was cocky and full of himself. But as she got to know him, she learned Jackie had a serious mind and—more important—respected that she had one, too. After they'd known each other for a year, they were deeply in love.

No matter what happens, this relationship is going to be one of the most important parts of my life.

Jackie's appeal crossed color lines. Author Myron Uhlberg wrote of how his deaf father connected with Jackie because they were both out of place in the world. Bette Bao Lord wrote a fictionalized memoir called *In the Year of the Boar and Jackie Robinson*, about how Jackie's courage helped her overcome her own barriers as a Chinese immigrant. Anyone who had ever been told they didn't belong, or who stood out for their differences, felt a connection.

And some fans loved Jackie simply because he was an exciting player to watch. He would get on base, take a lead, and dare the pitcher to make a throw. He was always a threat to steal. He would steal third base with two outs. He would steal home! Some fans compared him to baseball's all-time greatest base runner, Ty Cobb. Jackie's fearlessness on the base path lifted the rest of the team. They hit better because the pitchers were rattled and infielders were distracted.

Memorabilia

- Buddy Johnson record, *"Did You See Jackie Robinson Hit That Ball?"*

- Collectible cards

- Cover of *Time* magazine

- Jackie Robinson comic book

Excerpt text copyright © 2019 by Sandra A. Agard.
Excerpt illustrations copyright © 2019 by Artful Doodlers.
Published in the United States by Random House Children's Books,
a division of Penguin Random House LLC, New York.

TRAIL BLAZERS
HARRIET TUBMAN
A JOURNEY TO FREEDOM
I should fight for my liberty.
SANDRA A. AGARD

⋛ HARRIET'S ESCAPE ⋛

That night, Harriet went about her usual chores. John was hardly speaking to her these days, and they spent most evenings in silence. When she knew John was sound asleep, she got up quietly and helped herself to some ash cake (a type of bread), a piece of salt herring, and her wedding quilt.

Rather than set off into the woods, Harriet decided to head for Bucktown to the farm on the edge of the town. She was going to ask that white woman she had met by the road for assistance. It was a risky move—although the woman had said she'd help, Harriet couldn't know whether she'd really meant it, or how committed she would be to her offer once she discovered that Harriet was a runaway.

She uttered a quick prayer, walked toward the woman's door, and gently tapped on it. In the stillness of the night, the knock sounded so loud. The door opened, and the Quaker woman appeared. To Harriet's great relief, the woman nodded and asked Harriet to come in. She led Harriet into the kitchen and told her to sit down. She wrote two names on a piece of paper, then gave Harriet directions of where to go next.

The first stop, or station, on the Underground Railroad was another farm; Harriet couldn't miss it— there were two white posts with round knobs on them. The people there would give her food and clothing and keep her safe until it was time to move to the next place.

≥ FAME AND FORTUNE ≤

As she grew more famous, it became difficult for Harriet to make as many trips down South as before. Still desperate to help the Underground Railroad's efforts, in 1858 she began lecturing at locations all over the North. Her firsthand accounts of the Underground Railroad and its workings proved very popular, and she raised even more money to help fugitives, station masters, and conductors fighting to free slaves.

She was invited to speak in the parlor rooms of high society in Concord and Boston. In these anti-slavery speeches, Harriet told fascinating stories of her narrow escapes. Money poured in as more and more people heard about her amazing rescues.

≥ HARRIET'S STORIES ≤

One time, Harriet was traveling during the day in her home state of Maryland. She was wearing a large sunbonnet and kept her head bowed, but when she passed a former employer, Harriet worried that she would be recognized. Luckily, she'd just bought a couple of chickens at the market.

Thinking quickly, she opened the cage of chickens, which fluttered and squawked, causing an awful noise and diverting attention from herself.

On a different occasion, Harriet was traveling in a railroad car and noticed two gentlemen quietly discussing whether she was the woman on the Wanted poster at the station. Never one to panic, she simply picked up a newspaper and began to "read" it. Harriet Tubman was known to be illiterate—so this woman reading the paper studiously surely could not be the fugitive!

COMING SOON . . .

Albert Einstein

Beyoncé

Stephen Hawking

J. K. Rowling